BUSINESS STRATEGY EDITION 5

JOHN LOK

Introduction

In our business society, we are facing different kinds of business challenges in different countries business environment. However, in any organizations, staffs and employers also encounter different department difficulties, if we do not know how to find solutions or implement effective strategies to solve these organizational challenges. Our organizations will not achieve raise efficiencies or improve performance. So, if we can predict any kinds of challenges which will be possible to occur as well as we can know how to implement effective strategies to solve these problems. Consequently, we may avoid any challenges occur to cause our organizational failures.

In my this book, I shall attempt to give some opinions to solve any kinds of orgnizational challenges. I shall indicate any business environment challenge and explain the most effective strategies to attempt to solve these challenges. Readers can understand how and why that this kind of strategy which is the most effective solution to this organizational challenge in this organization.

Contents

Prologue

Table of content

Q1 How facility management influences airport and logistic organizational employee performance ? p.56-70

Q2 How facility management influences public service transport service performance ?

Q3 Can gather the choosing right data public transportation service station facilities asset and analytics, it can give recommendation to help any organization to boost service quality?

Q4 How Facility management influences employee Psychology to raise productive efficiency ?

Q5 Is empowerment one good method to raise employee himself/herself effort in order to improve productive efficiency in organizations ?

Q6 Can organizational facility environment factor influences new and old employees long term performance ?

Q7 Can efficient and effective interview psychological methods improve organizational performance ?

Q8 What is organizational efficient raising actual mean?

CHAPTER ONE

Strategy

Q1 How to implement hotel management strategy ?

Hotel management is really about overseeing every operation of the property. This requires knowledge of distribution strategy, finance, customer service, staff management, marketing, and more. In no way should any of these be treated as 'set and forget'. Hotel management is about constantly evaluating performance is every facet of the business and making necessary adjustments.

Ultimately effective hotel management will not only ensure your hotel stays in business, but is able to profit and grow over time. Think of the hotel as an ecosystem that will get healthier the better you manage it. As your hotel becomes more successful you can upgrade and charge higher rates, pay staff higher wages, and create an experience that guests want to come back for. It can take time to get everything right however. There are many skills you'll already possess but many others you need to learn along the way, or else hire staff that can provide the knowledge for you.

Hotel management definition

Definition of hotel management is that it's 'a field of business and a study, that tends itself to the operational aspects of a hotel as well as a wide range of affiliated topics. Such as: Accounting, administration, finance, information systems, human resource management, public relations, strategy, marketing, revenue management, sales, change management, leadership, gastronomy and more.'Clearly there's a lot to be aware of and many of these functions do require specialists. However not all properties have the luxury of hiring a full team of staff, so it's certainly not impossible to run a successful small hotel business without a range of degrees.

What does hotel management strategy mean? Hotel management strategy may include: service performance management, facility management, cost or expense control management three aspects. Service performance management main aims to let customers to feel the hotel's security is safe when they are living in the hotel, front office service, room service room, even, restaurant food delivery service, entertainment service, such as swimming, gym sport , tennis sport etc. different kinds of whole service can let customers to feel satisfactory as well as facility management service, e.g. swimming pools can let swimmers to feel safe when they are swimming, swimming pools water is warm and clean when they are swimming, swimming pools facility is new, or sport gym running machine, riding machine facility is safe to use and new sport facility can let them to feel to play when they use any kinds of sport tools facility, the hotel room's kitchen tools are clearn, enough provison, kitchen is clean, room is clean, e.g. beds, toilets, drinking cups, plates are clean and enough number provision, when fire occurrence, the stairs areas are large sizes to let many people run on the hotel staires when many customers are running down in the same time. All of any hotel facilities will let customers feel safe or new use in order to let them to feel comfortable to live in the hotel as well as control cost is the main aspect to assist the hotel how to avoid to expend excess expenditure per month. So, how to implement cost control strategy will influence any one hotel income. All of these three aspects may be any one hotel main considerable issues. How to implement effective strategies will be one important discussion issue as below:

Hotel facility management strategy

For hoteliers, hotel management is not one concept. It's hard to really say you've mastered hotel management when it comes with such a range of roles and responsibilities. Being able to adapt, meet challenges, and place yourself on a scale of personal growth is vital for a hotel manager.

There are always new strategies, traveller preferences, or industry technologies emerging that you have to keep track of. Even new roles within hotels and the hotel industry are being created that will affect the way one manages their property.This blog will take you through the major considerations to keep in mind regarding hotel management and throw some tips and ideas along the way, to help you run a better hotel business.

- How managing a hotel as an independent operator?

Hotel operations management: Inventory and revenue

The day to day operations of a hotel are pretty all encompassing. Is everything that guests need in order? Are staff and cleaning schedules organised? Is the occupancy rate where you'd like it to be? Obviously a core aspect of hotel management is to manage your rooms; or your inventory.

Effective inventory management for hotels involves both creating and managing demand, and maximising returns. The investment backing a hotel is tied up in its rooms and the returns can only be gained from selling those rooms optimally.

Here are some strategy basics:

1. Pricing strategy

By driving prices up during high peak periods and knowing how much to discount prices by to ensure rooms are rented during low peak periods, hotels can maximise their return. Through dynamic pricing, businesses can provide discounts and incentives in a controlled way during different seasons.

2. Distribution strategy

Hotels generally advertise their rooms through multiple channels, such as online travel agencies, to optimise reach and promote sales. Distribution management is essential and this involves calculating the minimum numbers of rooms needing to be sold for any given period by each channel. In doing so, you then have the ability to make informed choices regarding reallocation from cancellations or where to list spare rooms to maximise sales.

3. Market segmentation

Being aware of your hotel room visitor need market and the variable preferences, demands and affordability of different demographics are paramount to understanding how to price and distribute your room sales across the various channels. Not only does this help in managing your existing rooms, but it can also allow you to capture more of the market and increase sales and revenue. Flexibility is an important virtue required of hoteliers and being able to understand your clientele and adapt to their needs is vital to building loyalty and guaranteeing profitability.

Revenue management is another huge part of managing your hotel. How do your hotel get smore money coming in and achieve business goals? Smart revenue management and pricing strategies are needed if you want to optimise your Average Daily Rate . I shall recommend some hotel promotion methods as below:

1. Packages, promotions and extras

Packages are any rate that pairs the accommodation with an add-on; it could be free breakfast, free parking, or a ticket to a local event or attraction.Take a look at these methods to make sure your packages offer a unique experience.

Promotions are special rates that can change depending on:

The season or holiday period;

If the guest is a VIP; or,

You want to capitalise on an event.

You can get even more specific by offering things like mobile-only promotions.

Extras are an added expenditure that guests will only realise they want during the booking process. This might include items like champagne and chocolate stocked in their room, shuttle services from the airport, or activities like exercise classes. Extras are an added expenditure that guests will only realise they want during the booking process. This might include items like champagne and chocolate stocked in their room, shuttle services from the airport, or activities like exercise classes.

2. Events and tours

Selling tickets to local events, tours, or offering car rental is a good point-of-sale opportunity to increase your revenue per customer as well as providing a more satisfying experience for your guest.

3. Sell your hotel products

If you offer your guests the chance to buy your shampoo, bath and beach towels, art pieces, linen and so on, it can provide you with extra revenue and might even save you from the cost of replacing items that guests 'accidentally' pack with their own luggage when they depart.

4. Referrals and return business

If your guests give you positive feedback on completion of their stay, encourage them to share their experience with family and friends, and on social media to drive more bookings and brand awareness. You could also set guests up with a promotion code to get a discount the next time they stay. This encourages return business and helps you keep a consistent occupancy rate.

5. Accommodate flexible travellers

Some travellers don't have a set itinerary or allow themselves flexibility with their schedule, so take the opportunity to raise your occupancy and incremental revenue by offering guests a discount for an additional night's stay. Some mistakes have worse consequences than others and depending on the industry, backlash can range from minor to cataclysmic. The type of mistake you make will also have an impact on this. Did it just affect you, or did it also affect your customers?

● Designing hotel website promotion strategy

However, in the hospitality industry almost everything revolves around the customer, and they're the quickest party to point out any flaws. There's also plenty of times where you might simply self-sabotage and fail to get the most out of your business. Human fallibility prevents us from eliminating all our mistakes, but you can certainly look out for some common errors to avoid. I shall indicate some human avoidance mistakes on hotel website design and advertment skillful aspect to cause poor hotel room customer individual experience from your hotel website advertisement as below:

1. Failing to provide basic contact information

A beautiful looking hotel website with a fancy design and stunning features means nothing to the customer if they can't find your address or phone number on the homepage. The basics are something every hotel must get right before anything else. Travellers have all kinds of queries and many of them want to call to get instant clarification, and often people will be calling to make a booking so your phone number is an absolutely essential piece of information.

2. Website scarecrows – autoplay videos and music

Many people book holidays between the hours of 9AM – 5PM, i.e work hours. The last thing they need is for their computer to start blasting commercials or ditties around the office. The first thing they'll do is close your website and it's unlikely they'll return.

3. Incorrect use of social media

It's great to use social media as a marketing avenue but it's important you use it in the right way. You want traffic to be directed to your website and booking pages, not away from them. A common mistake hoteliers make is sending website visitors away to their social media channels immediately after a visitor has landed on the homepage. How many people are going to be coming back once they've been redirected to YouTube for instance?

4. Poor quality photos

There's really no point in investing in a great website design if the photos you integrate into the theme are lacking quality. Travellers want to see what they're paying for and if what they see is a grainy, blurry, or poorly framed image they won't be racing to open their wallets. Paying for high quality photography is worth every penny and you should update your images every couple of years, or every time you refurbish.

5. Downloads for simple information

Does anyone actually enjoy downloading a PDF to their phone or computer? The answer is probably no so why would you make a prospective guest do this? If a traveller wants to view the menu of your hotel restaurant for example, they should be able to do it on your website. Making them download documents is a conversion killer.

6. Connecting to the wrong distribution channels

When you connect to online travel agents manually or via a channel manager, it's still important to do some research. You have to look beyond the four or five biggest channels and find partners that most suit your target market.

7. Ignoring the potential of the local area

Guests are simply buying a hotel room when they come to stay at your hotel. For them, they're paying for an experience delivered by the destination. It would be silly for you not to take advantage of this. Make sure you partner with local businesses and run promotions and packages around local events and attractions.

8. Closing your ears (and mouth) to feedback

Reviews are one of the most important aspects to get right for your hotel. Customer satisfaction and brand reputation are vital if you want to keep the bookings coming in. The worst thing you can do is stay silent online when people leave reviews and feedback on sites like TripAdvisor or your social media pages. You need to respond diligently to both positive and negative reviews.

9. Not paying close attention to seasonality

The price people are prepared to pay for their hotel room will depend on the supply and demand trends over time. Seasonality matters, and you'll have to change rates a number of times during the year to reflect buying behavior and market conditions. This, together with the date and timing release of packages and promotions forms an integral part of your sales and marketing plan.

10. Lacking attention to detail in housekeeping

One of the most common complaints from guests is about dirty rooms or general uncleanliness of the hotel. There should never be any shortcutting when it comes to housekeeping and cleaning. Not only is it a healthy and safety issue, but you open yourself up to a flood of negative reviews. Of course, there are plenty of other pitfalls that could hit your hotel so you have to be constantly diligent and find ways to optimise your processes, reducing the risk of mistakes that could cost you money.

● Hotel and restaurant management strategy

Life gets even more complicated for hotels that also have a restaurant. Since managing a restaurant is a whole other kettle of fish. A study by Leonardo looked at what images travel shoppers viewed the most. Obviously the number one result was guest rooms but the second most viewed was restaurant photos.

This indicates that travel boils down to two primary needs; people want a nice place to sleep and they want a nice place to eat. Most of the time the hotel restaurant is a solid driver of revenue and an integral part of the hotel's identity, so it's ability to help market and sell your hotel should not be underestimated. Here are some reasons your restaurant will drive more bookings and how you can aid the process:

1. Individualise your restaurant

The first thing you need to do is to maximise the quality of your product by treating your hotel restaurant as a restaurant in its own right, rather than a glorified bar only accessible by guests. Turn your restaurant into a premium dining experience that focuses on the whole package including the food, lighting, music, decor, and wine lists. This way, your restaurant won't only be the bait to bring new customers in, but also an incentive for current guests to return when they revisit the area. At the same time it's important to remember who your customers are and understand what they want and what they can afford. Create a menu that will sell, not one you think is cool and trendy, and make sure the pricing is in alignment with the rest of your hotel. Using local produce will help with this.

2. Give your restaurant its own website

Don't let the physical setting of your restaurant deter you from creating a separate website for it. While it should also be featured on your hotel website, a dedicated restaurant website will help maximise revenue and potentially increase traffic to your hotel via page links.The restaurant website should feature large, high-resolution images and videos to showcase the food and decor. Hopefully, if guests land here and see they can also stay in the hotel, they'll be more convinced to stay and book direct.

By cross-referencing both lines of business you'll improve your search engine optimisation and maximise the traffic and conversions you receive. You should make sure everything is optimised for mobile devices and you could also include a direct link to your hotel's booking engine on your restaurant website.

By dedicating a separate website to your restaurant you'll be catering to consumer's need for relevant and distinctive content while also increasing your web presence. It's definitely worth the time and effort, especially if you use a smart intuitive website builder.

3. Make offers or give discounts

Consider offering different restaurant deals for different parts of the week to further encourage people to book with your hotel. Midweek you might advertise via social media or another medium giving away cheaper drinks or free desserts. On the weekend you might include a discounted three-course meal with a booking. As we know, managing a hotel is an extremely complex, stressful, and time-consuming task. The same can be said of running a successful restaurant. Combining both might seem like a fool's errand. And while there's definitely some risks involved in such an enterprise, there's also the opportunity for rich rewards at your hotel.

Hotel restaurant management: How you need to operate

Not only does a successful hotel restaurant have to serve and please your guests at your property, it has to stand on its own as a dining option for anyone in the local area. This is because many guests will want to explore the city and the many options available to them. So if you can't convince your guests to stay in for a meal, you have to attract other paying patrons. Who knows, some diners might even decide to make it a night and book a room directly through your front desk. For this to work the quality of your product has to be high. Your hotel restaurant has to individualise itself and offer a comprehensive dining experience. This means in addition to great food, you need to focus on lighting, music, decor and well thought out wine lists.

Things you need to consider include:

1. Hotel Space

How big will your restaurant attraction be relative to your hotel?

Different departments Staff number

How many patrons can you serve and how many extra staff will you need to oversee this?

2. Restaurent Food Menu

Will you create a menu that sells and is affordable or one that is cool and trendy? Make sure it's in line with who you expect to enter your restaurant.

3. Hotel Room And Food Packages

Obviously giving guests deals and discounts when they book a room direct with you will help increase restaurant traffic and revenue for your property.

● Hotel Restaurant And Hotel Room Bookings good relationship strategy

You should always reserve some tables for your own customers. If a guest walks down to eat and the restaurant is booked out by people not staying at the hotel, the response may be less than favourable.

The main issue is that if your restaurant is receiving poor reviews, it could be turning people off booking a room, no matter how amazing the rest of your hotel is. If it looks like the effort to produce the best possible experience is missing in the restaurant, travellers will assume the same for your whole business and look elsewhere. The same risk applies on the other side of the coin. If your hotel is derided for a poor experience and your occupancy is low, your restaurant could dwindle and die if it relies solely on business from outside the hotel walls.

Your hotel and restaurant have to work in harmony to keep each other strong.

Here are five tips to make your hotel restaurant a success:

1. Strike a balance between class and convenience

For guests already staying at your hotel your restaurant should be a quick and easy place to get a meal. They won't want to spend too much money, nor spend too much time waiting for food if they have other plans. On the other hand, diners coming for the restaurant alone will be expecting first-class ambience, food, and service.To keep everyone hotel customer feels happy and satisfactory when they are living in your hotel, you need to offer a simple but delicious menu that can be eaten in a comfortable setting that also promotes social interaction.

2. Give your restaurant its own website

While it should certainly be featured on your hotel website, a dedicated restaurant website will help maximise revenue and potentially drive extra traffic through your hotel via links. Cross-referencing both lines of business will improve your SEO and help maximise conversions and direct bookings. On your restaurant website, feature large high-resolution images and videos to showcase your food and decor. It will bring attractive and exciting website photos to persuade your potential hotel customers to choose to live your hotel.

3. Create a social media page for your restaurant

If your hotel restaurant has its own website it stands to reason it should have its own Facebook page too. This is especially true if regular events are hosted. Think live music on Friday nights, monthly wine tasting, or happy hours. It's also useful for posting pictures of your food and dining experience.

4. Offer deals and discounts

You can use different parts of the week and different mediums to drive customers to your restaurant. Before a guest arrives, email them a drink voucher for the restaurant bar. It's likely they'll also grab a meal. You might use social media midweek to promote cheaper drinks or free desserts with every meal order. On the weekend, you could offer a three-course deal when a guest makes a booking.

5. Hire talented hospitality staff

Given the unique challenge of running a restaurant, you need staff that are specifically trained to meet it. Give them the power to create the best possible restaurant experience for your hotel's guests. Hotels and restaurants both form a large part of the hospitality industry and customer service is vital to both. These businesses live and die by customer satisfaction because of the public exposure they're always open to. Guests are only too eager to share stories of their holiday or dining experience – both good and bad.

- Building good cooperative relationship between travel agents and your hotel in your country

Hotel management: Optimising your online travel agent profile. It's common knowledge hotels are at a disadvantage if they aren't engaging online travel agents to boost their distribution and sell rooms. The prominence of OTAs, such as Expedia and Booking.com, continues to grow and they're a proven resource for travellers who use them to discover a diverse range of accommodation options at the best price. Connecting to OTAs will help hotels increase visibility and maintain their occupancy. Your property may even rank higher on search engines – and yet the commission fee from OTAs can feel like a necessary evil if hotels want to accomplish this. However, to make sure you get the full benefit of OTAs and their reach, there's a number of steps you should follow to optimise your hotel's profile. Given your hotel is a brand, your marketing efforts should be consistent across all channels. Don't save your best images and content just for your website, make sure this is also on the OTA websites.

Similar to search engines such as Google, OTAs have their own algorithms for how your property will rank, meaning you need to pay close attention to the following tips:

Here are 6 easy steps to optimise your hotel's OTA profile:

1. Accurately manage your inventory

Because the availability of your rooms will fluctuate due to peak periods or seasonal changes, you need to maintain an accurate inventory across all OTAs to keep your occupancy rate high. Using a channel manager with pooled inventory is the best way to achieve this because travellers won't be disrupted by double booking issues or incorrect data.

2. Cleverly manage your rates and promotions

Guests don't simply use OTAs for a wide range of choice and inspiration, often they're looking for last minute deals and offers. If you have time-sensitive promotions they'll have more chance of being caught and you can more easily sell the remainder of your rooms. It's not hard to make alterations on OTAs to highlight a particular rate or capitalise on seasonal events to attract more guests to your property profile.

3. Carefully respond to reviews

While only 14% of consumers trust traditional advertising, 92% respect reviews on sites such as TripAdvisor. Reviews on OTAs are traditionally reliable because guests can only post a review after they've stayed at the property. However, only 36% of hoteliers respond to reviews on OTA sites. It's important to do an efficient job of managing online reviews.

4. Consider paid advertising

This doesn't have to be restricted to big and rich hotel corporations. It can also be a viable option for independent hotels on a pay-per-click basis. While paid advertising is no guarantee of more bookings, it will help make your property front-of-mind. If your content and aesthetic is strong enough, you should see a rise in revenue and your OTA ranking.

5. Focus on specific markets

Narrowing down your targets will mean you impact a lower volume of customers but you're also more likely to secure the bookings you want if you use certain time periods, events, geo-targeting or other methods to target specific audiences.

6. Understand your competition

It's vital to know who the similar players in your market are so you aren't significantly underselling or overselling your rooms. If you are, you won't be able to compete. On top of this, being aware of their activity may provide an opportunity to snare extra bookings. For example, changing rates could indicate the occupancy of a competitor or a promotion based on something you could also benefit from. There are specific data systems hotels can use to monitor competitors. With an optimised OTA profile, your hotel will not only gain bookings from third-party channels but direct traffic to your website should also increase, helping you to offset the commission fee you pay.

● Hotel restaurant food management strategy

To improve the way you manage your hotel, you have to think about everything and look for ways to save time and money, or increase efficiency. Even small changes can reap big rewards over the course of a financial year. Sticking with the theme of food, there's a big opportunity here. As humans, food represents our most essential connection to the planet and its resources. Yet environmental researchers often surmise that we place less value on food than we used to. Following US hotel kitchen indicates that hotel GDP information. You only have to look at numbers from Hotel Kitchen around food waste to understand their perspective:

In the US alone, an estimated 40% of all food is scrapped

American hotels serve food worth $35 billion each year

It's estimated that 40% of food in customer-facing businesses, such as hotels and supermarkets, goes to waste

How to control food waste in your hotel's kitchen

Fighting food waste at your hotel goes beyond feeding people and helping the environment – it also improves your property's bottom line. Do you really know how much food you throw away each week? Have you worked out its monetary value? Are staff and guests aware of your efforts to be more sustainable and properly manage food waste disposal? According to Hotel Kitchen, more than 90% of staff say they want to take action on tackling food waste. Guests are also becoming increasingly savvy with 60% of those surveyed saying they expect hotels to be actively reducing waste across their operations.

There may be steps your hotel restaurant can take to reduce waste:

1. Get buy in on food waste from your team

Create a team to take ownership of waste reduction and incentivise them. This should include a cook or chef and a kitchen porter (KP). Your KPs see what gets scraped off plates, while a chef will know how leftover ingredients can be better used in future menus.

2. Research waste management software to support processes

Conduct a waste audit, by dividing waste into categories and ensuring staff dispose of it in an appropriately-labelled container. There is weight-based software for this: basically a talking bin that records the weight of different categories of waste according to descriptions entered by staff on a touchscreen. The most well-known of these is probably the Winnow system, which its manufacturer claims typically saves operators 3-5% on food costs – a ROI of up to 10 times within a year. The challenges with using a system like this is that, it requires all waste to go into the same bin, leading to congestion in the kitchen or pot wash, and it can take time to input the data.

3. Assess raw ingredients vs. diners' plates

If conducting a waste audit manually, you'll need to at least split waste into raw ingredients and prepared waste that is left on diners' plates. Almost 10% of raw ingredients are wasted. This includes things like potato peelings and cauliflower leaves, which can be difficult to find a use for. Raw ingredients also covers kitchen prep mistakes. Some 35% of restaurant waste is left on diners' plates. This is most definitely higher in a hotel restaurant, where diners are less likely to take their leftovers home.

4. Asking staff for their frequent observations

Raw ingredients and diners' plates might be the two main categories, but make sure you have as many containers as you have space for. Record the waste, by weight, but also anecdotally. You'll learn more from staff comments: what did they find surprising? Was there an item plated but not eaten? Is there a garnish that customers commonly leave?

5. Following the 'less is more' approach

Assemble as many staff as possible to discuss the results, after a fortnight or a month. When it comes to prepared waste, you may find that it's a result of portion sizes being too large, in which case introduce strict portion controls, possibly using measure scoops that are colour-coded for different items. If lots of butter and preserve is left after breakfast service, consider buying in individual wrapped portions. Keep in mind that, unavoidable post-consumer waste can often be used by farmers as animal feed: all good content for your Instagram stories.

6. Obsessing over food and beverage expiration dates

If you discover that fresh items are going out of date, introduce a strict fridge rotation system and coloured stickers to identify which items to use first. Store new foods on the right fridge and existing on the left to maximise shelf life. Get this ingrained and replicate it in ambient storage areas for rice, herbs and spices, pulses and grains as well. Out of date ingredients can usually be donated to local food banks. Build a relationship with your local food bank operator and post about it on social media to boost your presence in the local community. This may lead to worthwhile involvement in charity events.

7. Sharpen up your kitchen team's knife skills
Meat carcasses should always be used for stock. If staff report that there is still a lot of meat left on bones, check that knives are being properly sharpened and that staff are trained to bone items efficiently. If staff lack butchery and fishmongers skills you'll save on waste by buying, for example, cubed chicken and filleted fish.

8. Using proper peelers for vegetables
Similarly, are staff prepping vegetables properly? You'll see less waste using peelers than knives for most fruit and root vegetables.

9. Allocating some space for composting
Raw vegetable waste can be composted if you have some outside space. A compost area can be simply constructed out of pallets. The resulting compost can be used to improve the soil on site or donated to local allotment groups. It can often be valuable to look at what businesses in other parts of your industry are doing, and seeing how you compare or what you might be able to employ in your own business strategies.

10. Getting customer service ideas from restaurants
There are similarities between service in restaurants and hotels, but also a few differences. Let's see how great customer service in restaurants translates to achieving guest satisfaction in hotels.

A great first step is turning 'service' into 'hospitality'
Service is basically about performing a task; doing something for someone. It denotes a mechanical action. On the other hand, hospitality is about making an impression on someone and going the extra mile to make their experience a memorable one. The interaction involved in hospitality is a genuine one and should be based on a caring attitude. Hospitality is something the best restaurants do extremely well. Customers will generally be served by one waiter their entire visit and will be made to feel like close friends or family, constantly attended to and conversed with warmly. Any requests will be responded to immediately. By the end of the meal, customers will look forward to coming back and seeing their waiter again.

In hotels, guests might interact with many different staff members throughout their stay, meaning they don't always get this personal connection. They may have to wait longer for services and might get frustrated when the staff member doesn't remember their preferences. The attentiveness of restaurants is certainly something hotels can try to replicate. Some things to try is to greet guests by name, get to know their interests, and don't delay when they want attention.

Giving guests a personalised experience at your hotel
A recent report shows full-service and fast food restaurants are revamping their menus and establishing more mobile ordering options, to the delight of customers. Restaurants are adapting their menus and technology to align with shifting consumer preferences. This looks at millennial tastes for fresh food, mobile ordering, and automated kiosks. The bottom line is that restaurants are working hard to please consumers in a way the customers are dictating, resulting in higher satisfaction.

Hotels need to do the same. New technology, both front and backend, needs to be explored if customer service is to improve. Again this comes back to hospitality and personalisation. Give each specific guest what they need. Even if you look at mobile check-in, it's not something everyone wants. Obviously some guests will be in a rush or tired from travel and simply want to get to their room as fast as possible. Others will be craving some human interaction. It's about what's convenient for the individual hotel guest. Technology should be able to help hotels in every regard. Think about how technology can improve the in-room experience, especially when it comes to speeding up room service or cleaning processes. Conversely, if backend tech that makes it easier to manage reservations and distribution is used, more time can be dedicated to guest experience.

Empower staff to solve their own problems

Nothing will frustrate a customer more than a staff member always needing to clear something with their manager. Not only does this take more time, but it makes the staff member look incompetent. Quality restaurants will take difficult or specific requests in their stride and provide customers with any special needs they require. If something goes wrong, their constant hands-on experience allows them to solve it, without the intervention of a manager. Again, it's done with a smile on their face because nothing is too much trouble for a valued customer.

Hotels need to train and empower their staff this way too. A great example is The Ritz-Carlton Hotel Company, where even hourly employees have permission to spend up to $2,000 per guest to solve any problem or dissatisfaction that may arise, without needing to ask for approval or involve management. And it's not the amount of money that's the point; it's the instant no-need-for-approval empowerment, which enables quick solutions for guests.

Hire the right traits in staff at your hotel

The very best restaurant staff show a passion for their job and authentic desire to make people happy. While the hospitality industry is one where skills can be learned on the job and thus standards may be lax, the approach taken to hiring staff must be taken very seriously.

To name just a few, some necessary traits a hotel should find it its staff include:

Empathy

Warmth

Conscientiousness

Enthusiasm

Charisma

● Hotel regular reports for effective hotel management strategy

Reporting on performance is essential to hotel management. You need to collect and analyse accurate data regularly to see where things are working, and what you need to improve on. There are a lot of different parts of the business you'll need reports on to inform your overall strategy. Most of them can be pulled from the systems that you're using such as your property management system and channel manager etc.

Some of the most important information your hotel different department managers need to track includes:

Channel performance

Website performance

Housekeeping
ADR – Average daily rate
Occupancy
RevPAR – Revenue per available room
TrevPAR – Total revenue per available room

Channel performance is key. You need to understand a number of factors about your booking channels. For instance, which channel is delivering the most reservations? Which channel is contributing the most overall revenue? Which channel has the highest cancellation rate? Which has the largest or smallest lead time?

The point is the more information you have about your channel performance, the more tweaks you can make to optimise your distribution mix. Cutting some channels and connecting others, or temporarily pausing, can enable you to maximise revenue.

Given how important direct bookings are, website performance is equally important. Since your booking engine can be included in channel performance you'll be able to see if direct bookings are down. Investigating your website is a good idea. How much traffic are you driving via organic and paid means? What pages are being visited the most? What's the conversion rate on calls to action? How many people are abandoning a booking part of the way through?

Housekeeping is extremely significant. Do you know how long it's taking to clean a room on average? How many guests are arriving to find their room isn't ready yet? Do you have enough cleaning resources or not enough? How efficient are staff?

This is all information you need to report on each and every month to see if your business is on an upward spiral or if standards are dropping. Through your property management and revenue management systems you can track occupancy, ADR, and many other metrics.

● Hotel management software technological strategy

Technology in the hotel industry continues to advance at a rapid pace and hotel management software (HMS) remains essential for hoteliers looking to improve the running of their business. With software, hotel operators can streamline their administrative processes and improve their overall hotel management system. The key to reaping the benefits of an effective hotel management software system is to select the right one for your property. It's critical that you know exactly what this hotel management technology is, and why it is important for you to implement it at your hotel.

What is hotel management software?

Hotel management software is technology that allows hotel operators and owners to streamline their administrative tasks while also increasing their bookings in both the short- and long-term. Your hotel management system is not only important for your own day-to-day operations, but it's a vital part of the overall guest experience. From the beginning of your guests' online booking journey until the completion of their stay and their feedback once they return home, it is necessary for your hotel management technology to enhance their experience with your brand.

Finding a hotel management system that offers the features you both need and want is necessary to effectively managing your hotel in a global economic climate.

The purpose of management systems for hotels

Management systems serve several purposes for both hotel operators who manage large chains as well as independent hoteliers. These include:

1. Managing bookings

Your property management system should help you efficiently and effectively manage your bookings. Neither you, nor your staff, should be tasked with manually inputting bookings and managing those across all your distribution channels. A property management system should automate the booking process for you, allowing you to escape the back office and focus more on interacting with your guests. In addition, it significantly reduces the risk of overbooking your rooms, which directly improves the guest experience at your property.

2. Direct bookings

It should allow you to actively drive direct bookings to your website. Travellers today are more apt to book online than they are to call to finalise bookings or partner with a travel agent. Direct bookings allow you to maximise the revenue that you generate per booking. You should only consider software that integrates with an online booking engine.

3. Channel management

Hotel management technology should allow you to easily implement your distribution strategy. Creating partnerships with different types of agents in the industry, such as OTAs and GDSs, is necessary to survive in a competitive, global climate. Managing hotel with software that offers a channel manager will allow you to create and implement a diverse distribution strategy that continually drives bookings.

4. Hotel website

Your hotel administration department software should help enhance your online presence. Your hotel management system is only effective if your guests can reach your brand. Choosing a program that offers a web editor or website creator will allow you to create a clean, appealing and user-friendly website that will encourage guests to book a stay at your property.

Benefits of hotel management technology

When you are selecting hotel management technology for your property, you should consider the many benefits that this system will offer you, including:

1. Reduce time spent on administrative tasks

You hotel can minimise the amount of time spent on administrative tasks. The right hotel management system will do a lot of the work for you, allowing you to focus your efforts and your energy on the big picture. The technology should also provide you with valuable data on how your employees perform their duties and how this affects employee retention, satisfaction and productivity. In today's fast-paced travel environment, it's critical that you automate as many tasks as possible. A property management system can help you tremendously with that.

2. Increase your online presence

Your hotel can increase your brand presence online. Management software that is integrated with your website builder will allow you to accept direct online bookings and develop a user-friendly website. Naturally, this will increase your relevance in the search engine results and allow more travellers to discover your property during their online booking journey.

3. Build relationships with guests

Your hotel will develop a better rapport with your target market segment, while also identifying new markets to tap into. The types of travellers who have always loved staying at your property will appreciate the improved experience. In addition, your new technology will allow you to reach out to new markets that would not have otherwise discovered your brand.

4. Manage your distribution

Your hotel will improve your reach throughout the industry. With a property management system in place that integrates with a channel manager, you will be able to advertise across many channels whilst maintaining rate parity. From the large OTAs and GDSs to individual retail travel agents, you can provide real-time booking information to your agents that will drive bookings.

5. Manage your hotel revenue and cost expenditure control

Your hotel can implement a beneficial revenue management strategy. Using innovative pricing tools that allow you to create a flexible room pricing strategy, you can maximise the revenue that you generate per room at any given moment. Pricing your rooms right is the key to succeeding in this competitive industry, and having these tools available can help you significantly.

6. Increase room bookings

Your hotel will ultimately increase your large , middle and small size room number bookings. At the end of the day, the point of every feature within your hotel management business solution is to boost the bookings that you get at your hotel. Whether your hotel wants to increase your off-season bookings or you want to expand your offerings to new market segments, you will be successful if you select the right hotel management software for your property.

● Hotel property facility management strategy

The first aspect, is your hotel safe facility system. Managing a hotel isn't all about managing the physical property, it's also about managing intangible things like reputation. Any hotel facility issues may influence hotel customers how feel your hotel service performance, for example, when your hotel customers are living in your hotel rooms, during this living period, they feel your hotel fire system is not safe, it will influnece that they choose to reduce room booking living days because they are afraid fire occurs can cause their death. So, any hotel floor fire safe property management facilities will influence any one customer makes booking room days decision whether they can extend days or shorten days to live in your hotel.

Another aspect, is your hotel online booking facility system. It's very simple. Hospitality businesses such as hotels are at risk if they don't focus attention on their online reviews and take control of their reputation management. As more and more guests turn to one another for advice on where to stay in cities around the world, the effectiveness of traditional hotel advertising is declining – while the impact of online hotel reviews is on the rise.

Failure to monitor, manage and respond to feedback will skew your hotel management strategy to issues that are unimportant to customers, as well as provide unhappy customers with ammunition for negative feedback on travel and social media sites. It can be difficult for an individual to get through their lives without significant episodes being recorded on social media channels, let alone a hotel to exist without the blemish of social media complaints.

As the impact of online bookings and digital feedback continues to rise, the importance of reputation management rises with it. Yet while online reputation management is a trend across the hospitality sector, it is still considered an indulgence by some independent hoteliers. Part of this rationale is driven by the confusion around how to deal with both positive and negative feedback online. So here are some standard ways hoteliers can deal with online reviews – regardless of sentiment:

The most feared of all feedback online is a negative review

However, audiences are particularly savvy in determining the value of feedback, not just because the "voice" of the author is on display, but because audiences often apply a filter to their reading of any review. Consciously or subconsciously, they consider the value of any commentary, as well as the relevance of a comment to their own experiences and preferences. So a comment on the convenience of a hotel location to an equestrian events venue will be of potential importance to horse-lovers, yet entirely irrelevant to many other potential guests. Where a rational negative comment is posted, hotels do have options on how to respond.

Acknowledge and Action

For a genuine, reasoned negative comment on customer experience, it is best for hotels to respond in a timely manner (within 72 hours of posting), acknowledging the issue and describing how it will be addressed. Ideally, a follow up post will occur after actioning the issue, and showing how the experience will not be repeated. This is by far the best possible response to negative feedback, because online audiences are far more willing to value action and positive changes in behaviour, than think poorly of the initial negative experience.

Apologise and Compensate

For a negative comment which illustrates an experience that was difficult or impossible to avoid, an appropriate response is to apologise for the poor experience and to privately offer either monetary compensation, or discounts on future bookings. While this is unlikely to totally satisfy the customer with the stated poor experience, it will indicate to other customers, the prioritisation of customer experiences at the hotel. It's important to take compensation offline where possible to avoid inviting those like to complain for free stuff.

Apologise and Thank

For negative comments that focus on pedantic details, the most appropriate response is an apology for the experience and an acknowledgement that this feedback will help shape your hotel's future guest experience strategy. This is far more useful than a response which states that the comment will be passed to a customer service team, because the customer already believes that service is the problem at the property.

How to thank hotel guests for their positive feedback

While most organisations are thrilled with the prospect of positive reviews, an abundance of rave reviews can be just as suspicious to audiences as a series of negative reviews. Therefore, positive reviews also need a response.

Be Humble

Where a positive review is excessive and perhaps gushing, it is wise for firms to thank the guest for their enthusiasm, but to also acknowledge areas where you are attempting to improve. This reinforces commitment to customer service.

Be Delighted

Where positive feedback is sincere and reasoned, the best response for hotels is to express delight and appreciation for the feedback and the desire to serve again in future. This is the easiest response to deliver, but is often the least fulfilled.

Be Appreciative

Where feedback is predominantly neutral, but some aspects are highlighted as being of particular value, it is advisable for hotel managers to express thanks for the feedback and to request further advice on how the organisation could improve in specific areas. Again, try to take this conversation offline with an email or personal phone call. This enables more considered feedback to follow the initial post.

● Reputation management strategy

Reputation management is often considered difficult or time-consuming. Yet the results of research into the importance of reputation management are unarguable: the value of reputation management is substantial and growing. Understanding how to respond to feedback is not just a competitive advantage, but potentially a means of ensuring your hotel stays in business. Your hotel can easily turn complaints around and win hotel guests back – and these basic reputation management responses are your first line of defence.

Hotel property management software

Selecting the right hotel software is critical, particularly in a world where consumers are relying more heavily on their devices with each passing day. An investment this important to your overall success as a hotel operator requires you to do some research.

These are seven questions that you should ask your hotel tech provider as soon as possible:

1. How does your hotel product maintains its relevance in the hospitality industry?

While the core of a technology system may remain the same over time, the reality is that any product geared specifically towards the hospitality industry will need to adapt to changing trends and preferences from travellers. You need to ask this question so you have an understanding of how your technology will help you grow along with the industry.

2. How often can your hotel expects upgrades for your platform?

No piece of technology is perfect, and the best hotel technology providers will make sure that regular updates and upgrades are available for their clients. It's important to have an understanding of how often these upgrades will be available, and how you will be able to successfully implement the upgrades.

3. What level of customer service will I receive from your company?

Unfortunately, far too many hotel technology providers focus on hard sales tactics without much support after the purchase is complete. You will want to verify with your provider that there will be ways to contact and work with staff after the technology has been installed at your hotel.

4. Is your hotel platform secure?

Security should be a top priority of your hotel technology provider. You will want to ask about the details regarding their security features, as it's imperative that both your data and your guests' data is secure.

5. How easily can your hotel personalise your systems?

Hotel technology providers need to offer you a versatile system that includes not only the generic features that are necessary for any hotel, but also the adaptable features that allow you to personalise the platform for your particular brand. Ultimately, your investment in technology needs to result in a system that works specifically for your hotel.

6. What reporting features are available?

When your hotel begin your search for the right hotel technology, you will likely focus first on the property management system. However, you will want to discuss additional features that also are available, with some of the most important being the reporting features. Verify that you'll be able to run detailed reports using live data, as this is the only way to ensure that you can grow your brand.

7. How can your hotel accesses the hotel technology system once implemented?

Be sure that you are investing in a system that allows you to run your hotel from anywhere. You need hotel technology that is optimised for all devices, including smartphones and tablets.

Benefits of a hotel management system

When you are selecting hotel management systems for your property, you should consider the many benefits they'll offer you, including:

1. Reduce time spent on administrative tasks

Your hotel can minimise the amount of time spent on administrative tasks. The right hotel management system will do a lot of the work for you, allowing you to focus your efforts and your energy on the big picture. The technology should also provide you with valuable data on how your employees perform their duties and how this affects employee retention, satisfaction and productivity. In today's fast-paced travel environment, it's critical that you automate as many tasks as possible. A property management system can help you tremendously with that.

2. Increase your hotel online presence

Your hotel can increase your brand presence online. Management software that is integrated with your website builder will allow you to accept direct online bookings and develop a user-friendly website. Naturally, this will increase your relevance in the search engine results and allow more travellers to discover your property during their online booking journey.

3. Build relationships with guests

Your hotel will develop a better rapport with your target market segment, while also identifying new markets to tap into. The types of travellers who have always loved staying at your property will appreciate the improved experience. In addition, your new technology will allow you to reach out to new markets that would not have otherwise discovered your brand.

4. Manage your hotel distribution

Your hotel will improve your reach throughout the industry. With a property management system in place that integrates with a channel manager, you will be able to advertise across many channels whilst maintaining rate parity. From the large OTAs and GDSs to individual retail travel agents, you can provide real-time booking information to your agents that will drive bookings.

5. Manage your hotel revenue

Your hotel can implement a beneficial revenue management strategy. Using innovative pricing tools that allow you to create a flexible room pricing strategy, you can maximise the revenue that you generate per room at any given moment. Pricing your rooms right is the key to succeeding in this competitive industry, and having these tools available can help you significantly.

6. Increase bookings

Your hotel will ultimately increase your bookings. At the end of the day, the point of every feature within your hotel management business solution is to boost the bookings that you get at your hotel.

Hotel property management system

All hotels need some variation of a property management system (PMS). However they come in many different forms and are not all created equal. There are still properties trying to manage their business in a traditional way with books and ledgers, others are using server-based systems, while many used web-based systems.

One of the most valuable things to a hotel manager is time, and money of course. The first two systems listed are a drain on both time and finances, while the latter has obviously become the optimal way to manage hotel operations. Cloud-based PMSs are a superior way to automate and accelerate all the important processes at your hotel such as taking and confirming bookings, managing reservations, generating bills and reports, check-in/out, room transfers, checking/editing availability, guest communication, the list goes in. Cloud-based technology can handle all these tasks with ease because of its ability to deeply integrate with channel managers, booking engines, and revenue management systems. Despite this, there are still concerns over the validity and cost effectiveness of cloud-based PMSs.

Here are five common property management system myths and why we think they're unfounded?

1. You think cloud-based technology is confusing or hard to use

Because it's intangible and seemingly floating in the air, some hotel managers believe using cloud technology will be hard to learn and too confusing to keep track of. The opposite is true. A PMS allows you to keep everything in one place and it can never be lost. You can access your data from any location so long as you have the Internet. The many tasks that you perform using multiple programs or books can be done from one central location with a fully integrated PMS. This also means you can collaborate better with other staff who need access to the same information.

2. You worry that sensitive data is insecure and vulnerable

While the information in your cloud PMS isn't kept under lock and key it is encrypted and backed-up. Nothing is stored 'onsite' so even if your computer breaks or your laptop is lost, your data will remain accessible to you. With data in the cloud you don't have to worry about viruses or bugs, and hacking is much less likely to succeed thanks to firewalls and authentication gateways.

3. Your current software works just as well as cloud-based technology

It's unlikely this is true and even if it is, it won't be for long. Cloud software is constantly being updated and evolved meaning users automatically get the benefits included in their monthly fee. If your current server isn't updated, it becomes slow and vulnerable, while updating it requires extra time and greater cost that has to be done too regularly.

4. You believe a web PMS is only suitable for large hotels

The reality is that smaller or independent hoteliers are often stretched thinner than anyone. With less staff and more responsibility, the time and hassle saved by using a cloud-based PMS is vital and could be the difference between getting the bookings needed for maximum occupancy or losing revenue on empty rooms.

5. You think hotel technology is too expensive

Cloud-based systems are actually very cost effective. You never require any additional hardware, backup solutions, licensing, updates, fixes. There's also no lengthy setup process and with the time you save using it, more resources can be directed towards increasing guest experience and revenue streams. Overall a cloud-based PMS will give you more control over your hotel business, with:

List of hotel property management systems may include as below:

There are literally hundreds of property management systems on the market. The most important aspect when choosing one is to ensure it's easy to use, has all the functions you need, and that it is able to integrate with your other important systems, such as your channel manager.

Some popular examples you might come across include:

Little Hotelier

Mews

Sirvoy

CloudBeds

Frontdesk Anywhere

eZee Frontdesk

Hotelogix

Maestro

OPERA

Avvio

Online booking engine

Essential if your hotel wants to capture direct bookings and reduce the commission you pay to online travel agents (OTAs). The majority of travellers will visit your hotel website even if they discover your property on an OTA.But if you're looking to capitalise on this traffic, your booking engine needs certain features beyond booking as a minimum including:

Seamless online experience for your guests via a customised, two-step booking process. Multi-language and currency capabilities to convert guests from around the globe. Mobile-friendly and Facebook-compatible to reach travellers on-the-go. Upselling capability so you can offer a more personalised stay for your guests. However your hotel booking engine can be a much more powerful tool that you can customise to suit any marketing strategy, allowing your business to maximise its revenue.

Ensure your hotel gets as much value as possible out of your booking engine by following these steps:

1. Prioritise booking engine and website integration

Seamless integration between booking engine and website will make a guests booking experience so much easier. It will be more responsive to mobile, put less pressure on you to design the look of your booking engine, and will maintain your branding throughout the entire booking process. All of this will enhance the trust your customers have in your hotel.

2. Create a strong foundation for search engine optimisation

While not directly related to your booking engine, SEO is vital. If your website isn't optimised for SEO it won't matter how amazing your booking engine is, you won't be attracting sufficient traffic to drive bookings.

3. Implement urgency messages

Urgency messages do exactly what they imply; invoke urgency in the shopper. By drawing attention to rates through urgency messages you can make your guests think they are in danger of missing out, or else getting something other customers aren't. They're a great way of speeding up the booking process and increasing conversions. Examples include 'Book now, pay later!' or 'Only two rooms left!'.

4. Use promo code banners

If you're running a promotion, you want guests to notice it. Display a prominent promo banner on your website using your booking engine so guests can easily view and select applicable dates and benefit from the promotion.

5. Set up an early-bird rate

By selling discounted early-bird rates you can improve your short-term cash flow by collecting full prepayment from the booker. You can control when to flag an early-bird rate via your booking engine extranet.

6. Introduce last-minute rates

Setting attractive last minute rates are good for increasing your short-term occupancy or filling any remaining rooms. Offset the rate by taking a high deposit to limit the amount of cancelled bookings or no-shows. Clearly display these and use them in conjunction with urgency messages.

7. Entice guests with a stay pay deal

Maintain your occupancy by increasing the length of your guests stay. Offer them a discount for one or more of their dates, clearly indicating the price difference and encourage them to book additional nights. Make sure you have control over what night is to be discounted; first, last, cheapest etc.

8. Interest guests in package deals

Packaging up extras like entry to events, attractions, or restaurants gives guests a one-stop shopping experience that they enjoy. Offer options guests can't find on OTAs and again entice them to stay longer. If used intelligently a booking engine can be a hotel marketing and branding tool that will incentivise guests to become loyal to your hotel, further increasing your direct bookings and revenue in the future.

Hotel room management software: Channel managers

A channel manager is a tool that will allow you to sell all your rooms on all your connected booking sites at the same time. It will automatically update your availability in real-time on all sites when a booking is made, when you close a room to sale, or when you want to make bulk changes to your inventory. There's a lot more to a channel manager than simply making life easier for when updating your rates and availability. You can use it to perform many tasks when managing your hotel and its benefits are two-fold in how it can increase bookings and revenue, and enable long term business planning.

Take a look at this comprehensive list of how a channel manager can be used to benefit a hotel.

1. Increase online bookings

With telephone and walk-in bookings on the decline and online bookings on the rise, a channel manager places you in the best position to take advantage of this new traveller booking habit. Connect to more online channels, where more travellers than ever are locking in their stays.

2. Increase hotel revenue

Given a channel manager displays live rates and availability across all your channels at the same time, and updates automatically you can accept bookings faster and almost eliminate the chance of double bookings. In addition, the data you can analyse from your channel manager can ensure your rates are always optimised and you're using the most lucrative channels.

3. Reduce the risk of overbookings

Without a channel manager, you're forced to split your inventory between channels and risk double-bookings or failing to reach full occupancy. Pooled inventory and automated updates of availability and rates in real time means guests can only ever book a room that is actually available.

4. Improve brand recognition

A powerful channel manager will provide two-way unrestricted access to hundreds of booking channels where travellers who would never hear of you can now make reservations at your property. It also makes OTAs more likely to accept your listing because they can be sure your inventory will always be accurate.

5. Boost direct bookings

It may seem illogical but it's true! Many travellers will discover your property first on an OTA, but they want to learn more about you before they book. Often they will visit your website and then make the decision to book their stay. So you get a direct sale, but it was born on the OTA site – resulting in greater profit for your hotel. This is known as the billboard effect.

6. Remove manual processes

Manual data entry is time-consuming and frustrating, we all know that. If you were to use a channel manager and remove this friction, you'd realise just how much more productive you can be. Anything that has to be put on hold can now be prioritised to improve your business.

7. Create a seamless, integrated tech stack

Instead of being required to update information in multiple extranets, a channel manager can integrate with your property management system, central reservation system, or revenue management system as well as your booking engine to create a central control system for the entirety of your hotel's operations. Some channel managers, like SiteMinder, also have a unique connection to Airbnb. Although boutique hotels have already been using Airbnb for some time, there hasn't been a solution for them to manage this channel in conjunction with other partners such as online travel agents – until SiteMinder's partnership.

8. Transform into a powerful business platform

A good channel allows complete transparency of data across all systems and channels, meaning you can use the received information to see which channels or rooms are performing the best. This means you can constantly update your business strategy. Look at reports such as channel yield and channel analysis and your reservation trends to see where things are going right – or wrong!

9. Reduce reliance on traditional booking channels

There's certainly no suggestion that you should leave behind traditional methods such as taking reservations over the phone or via walk-ins. It can be very profitable to save some of your inventory for these methods. However, using a channel manager will ensure you don't have to worry about filling your rooms in this manner. Connecting to a significant number of online booking sites will ensure your occupancy always remains steady.

10. Keep everyone on the same page

Quality channel managers are very easy to use and hotels will regularly have multiple staff members using the system. If the main user is going away or won't be available to make updates they can easily mark important dates in the system so everyone is aware if they need to change a rate or a close a room etc. For example, they may mark school holiday periods so rates can be increased during these peak times.

Hotel management apps technology

In order to enhance productivity at your hotel, you must first ensure you and your team are as organised as possible. This may be easier said than done when you have emails arriving non-stop, content to post and people to manage . Technology has evolved to solve almost any problem. There are many apps in the market to help with everyday challenges. Organised teams get more done and having everything under control also gives you a better grip on the overall success of the business.

Here are five hotel apps to help stay on top of hotel management:

1. Pocket

Have you ever come across interesting articles, videos or websites and ended up forgetting about them? Whenever you find something you want to view later, you can add it to your Pocket – an application and web service for managing reading lists. You can save content directly from your browser or from apps like Twitter, Flipboard, Pulse and Zite. Once saved to Pocket, the list of content is visible on any device (phone, tablet or computer) with access to your account – online and offline helping you share interesting articles with your hotel's team.

2. Astro

If a large part of your day-to-day duties includes sending and receiving emails, Astro will help you focus on what is most important. Astro brings along email and calendar features, powered by an Artificial Intelligence (AI) assistant, which will prioritise your emails, tell you what to follow up on, and help you clean up your inbox. Astro also adds reminders, snoozed emails, and scheduled emails to your calendar, so you can get a complete view of your day. You can also customise the emails you send with Open Tracking, Send Later, Custom Signatures, and much more.

3. Google Calendar

One of the most important parts of management is time management and having your calendar with you on the go can be crucial. Stay on track with your appointments and tasks with Google Calendar. Your events or any meeting requests received via Gmail can be automatically added to your calendar and you'll spend less time managing your schedule. Add images and maps to your appointments, and access your schedule for the day, week and month from any device at any time. You can also gain visibility of your team's work schedule and share your calendar view with them so you can make the most of your day.

4. Trello

Stay up to speed with your team projects using Trello – an easy, free, flexible, and visual way to manage and organise workflow. Trello is divided in boards, with lists representing the workflow. For example, you can have your Social Media Marketing board and inside the lists: To Do, Doing and Done. Every list has cards, representing tasks containing relevant information. For example, the New Years 7 Nights Promotion card will contain the specification of this promotion, such as due date, hotel team members that need to follow the task, checklists and more. As tasks progress along the way, the card will navigate to the next list. With Trello you have a clear and real-time view of the stage your project is at and you'll never lose track of them.

5. Evernote

If sometimes you feel the need for a second brain, meet Evernote – an app designed for note taking, organising tasks lists, and archiving. You can collect everything that matters in one place and find it when you need it, fast. Capture, organise, and share notes from any device and always keep your best ideas in sync and only a click away.

Evernote is not a simple note taking app, you can enhance your notes with links, checklists, tables, attachments, and audio recordings. Even handwritten notes are searchable. From initial brainstorm to finished project, Evernote will give you productivity bliss.

Apps the key to establishing self-service experiences

It's no secret modern-day travellers are becoming more accustomed to hyper-personalised and streamlined service from their hotels. In fact, if the hotel is going to deliver on its promise of quality, your guests expect a personalised and convenient experience.

Hotels can adapt to this growing need by prioritising data, technology, and connectivity. It's important to know what guests want, and also how to provide the appropriate services through hotel systems and applications. The tradition of limiting service and interaction to just your hotel staff and physical property is being outgrown by the ability of technology to automate and make many processes easier for guests. Where travellers once expected to be greeted by a front desk operator, they might now prefer the self-service experience that mobile check-in offers. Given the average person wastes an hour each week waiting in line, it's no surprise that self-service is catching on.

The self-service approach allows staff to be less transactional and focus on establishing genuine connections with guests. With technology in place, hotel employees will no longer be confined to stationary positions within the lobby or left to guess what guest expectations might be. For a better idea of the trends in this area and the enabling power of technology and connectivity, we spoke to four hotel applications to get their perspective.

Being able to adapt, meet challenges, and place yourself on a scale of personal growth is vital for a hotel manager. Hotel management is about overseeing every operation of the property. This requires knowledge of distribution strategy, finance, customer service, staff management, marketing, and more. Effective inventory management for hotels involves both creating and managing demand, and maximising returns. Revenue management is another huge part of managing your hotel. How do you get more money coming in and achieve business goals?

In the hospitality industry almost everything revolves around the customer, and they're the quickest party to point out any flaws. Good management eliminates as many mistakes as possible. Hotel management sometimes also requires the management of a restaurant.

Turn your hotel restaurant into a premium dining experience that focuses on the whole package including the food, lighting, music, decor, and wine lists. This way, your restaurant won't only be the bait to bring new customers in, but also an incentive for current guests to return when they revisit the area.

Similar to search engines such as Google, OTAs have their own algorithms for how your property will rank, meaning you need to pay close attention to how you build your profile on them. Fighting food waste at your hotel goes beyond feeding people and helping the environment – it also improves your property's bottom line. Reporting on performance is essential to hotel management. You need to collect and analyse accurate data regularly to see where things are working, and what you need to improve on. Hotel management software is technology that allows hotel operators and owners to streamline their administrative tasks while also increasing their bookings in both the short- and long-term.

Managing a hotel isn't all about managing the physical property, it's also about managing intangible things like reputation. There are many apps in the market to help with everyday challenges. Organised teams get more done and having everything under control also gives you a better grip on the overall success of the business.

● Keys to an effective hotel distribution strategy

How to increase your hotel's occupancy rate

Effective revenue management strategies for hotels

Essential strategies to increase your hotel room sales

Facility management, or FM, is a broad discipline that includes a variety of industries, from food to technology, manufacturing to e-commerce and beyond. But, though the core of each business may be completely different from even its closest competition, successful facility management practices are easily interchangeable from enterprise to enterprise. As a matter of fact, it is one of the only job titles that can be found in, basically, any small to large organizations, including public entities, like schools and hospitals, to private businesses, like those that manage their inventory in warehouses.But, reciprocal tendencies aside, facility management procedures and techniques must be highly-specialized for the business in which they are being used. Because the discipline covers complex specifics, including business continuity planning and even fire safety, it's key that your organization offers a holistic outlook on its facility management procedures.

● The Core Competencies of Hotel Facility Management strategy

According to the International Facilities Management Association (IFMA), facility management is an interdisciplinary practice that "considers the coordination of people, place, process, and technology." Broken down, this means that a facility manager is responsible for the success of the all facets of the facility, including organization, safety, security, and maintenance, along with the key, everyday operational practices. Facility Management Core Competencies

It may seem like an overwhelming job to put on one person or one small team – and it is an overwhelming job – but what's important to remember is the fact that facility management is just one aspect of what makes a healthy business. Simply put, all necessary departments must work with facility managers to build a business' overall success.

Safety – It's the facility management team's job to ensure the safety of all of the employees and customers occupying the property. This responsibility spans all possible environmental health and safety issues, particularly ones that concern the building and its equipment, specifically. Failure to do so can mean serious business in the form of fines, lost business, or even prosecution if it was deemed that the manager or business' negligence caused casualties or permanent environmental damage. Fire, for example, is usually right at the top of the radars of facility managers because it's a preventable tragedy that, when prepared for sufficiently, can save lives and valuable inventory. A thorough facility management team can protect its company best by guaranteeing that all parts of the facility are up-to-code, its employees are trained well, and all permits and certificates are completely valid. This function entails everything from safe and efficient lighting to flooring choices.

Security – In regards to importance, second to safety is facility security, yet another important piece of the puzzle in which the facility management team must answer to. Though larger companies or ones with particularly pricey inventory or equipment might make the wise choice to outsource its security needs in the form of a private firm, it's still the role of the facility manager to ensure that the firm performs competently. Technology advancements like biometrics and wearables are making it possible to maintain strict access control for high-security areas, but it's up to facility managers to stay on top of these developments and make smart security technology investments. In addition to general safety, it's also important that the facility management team has the technological know-how to safeguard and maintain its priciest hardware. This role is a key one as it doubly affirms that assets are protected just as closely as the safety of the community.

Maintenance and Inspections – No matter the focus of the organization, one of the most heedless things that a facility management team can do is slack off on its building maintenance duties. Every part of the building, including installed machinery such as HVAC systems, must be maintained by the facility management team. Because some facilities contain countless elements that need regular maintenance, establishing and following strict maintenance schedules helps to ensure that all moving and permanent parts of the facility stay up-to-date and working well into the future. Along with general maintenance, inspections are also something that facility management teams must always be ready for. They can prepare the business by conducting internal inspections, as needed, for the many formal regulatory inspections they might incur annually. Of course, the team must also take into account any time the facility undergoes a major change in hardware, level of inventory, or capacity – and, they must also keep their eyes on all changes in laws that could affect their current procedures.

Business Continuity Planning – Part of leading an effective facility management team means planning for "worst case scenarios." This means that each team must sit down with the powers that be to come up with a plan in case disaster strikes and the business can't afford to shut down operations. For example, let's say that a community college endures a major fire and the authorities have deemed the entire main building a total loss. The community college is currently in the middle of a semester which it can't cut short – this is a situation where prior business continuity planning is key. If this were done in the aforementioned scenario, the facility management team would have already come up with alternate locations to hold classes and operate the organization's administrative duties. In addition to the new venue, the team would have already made a solid plan for the temporary facility's security, maintenance, and hardware needs.

Daily Operational Duties – In addition to serving as the safety and security liaisons for the facility, it's also important that facility management teams are organized to handle the inherent day-to-day challenges that might arise. Depending on how the given organization is structured, this can mean anything from mending a leaky roof in the women's restroom to even fixing a jammed fax machine.

Maintenance Operations

No matter the size of the organization, it's key that the higher-ups bring on a facility manager that can hire or outsource a reliable, competent team. And, because not every company is filled with safety-minded individuals, it is the job of this manager to act as an advocate for the workers and/or customers that occupy their facility. Having this level of tenacity and attention-to-detail in the facility management spectrum is necessary – in fact, it can save a business or even a life.

Operations and Management Strategies

The current presiding global facilities management organization, the International Facility Management Association, calls for these leaders to take a more tactical and shrewd approach when it comes to protecting the future of their business' properties. In the IFMA's Strategic Facility Planning white paper, the organization makes a call for facility managers to carry out SFP (strategic facility planning) as it "helps to avoid mistakes, delays, disappointments, and customer dissatisfaction." In addition to the aforementioned safety and maintenance-heavy responsibilities, the IFMA wants managers to begin looking beyond their normal duties so that they can better aid in the efficiency of their organizations.To do this effectively, managers must compile two things: 1) a strategic facility plan and 2) a master plan for the facility. Let's take a look at how each one can better strengthen the overall productivity of the business:

Strategic Facility Plan (SFP) – In order to compile a comprehensive SFP, the IFMA urges managers to first become acquainted with three very important things: the core values or changing values of the organization and how facilities must reflect the values, the compiling of an in-depth analysis of the facility, including location, capability, and condition, and, finally, a fundamental understanding of how the organization's goals might make for the ramping up or down in regards to facilities. If the manager can confirm each and every one of these benchmarks with the appropriate departments and find a way to support their organization's ambitions while carrying out effective day-to-day practices, then they will be acting as a truly "strategic" support system. This blend of "current" and "future" allows for all parties involved to grapple with changes as they come in the most effective manner possible.

Facility Master Plan – Any facility manager should already be constantly re-working their facility's master plan, a framework that looks at the "physical environments that incorporate the buildings," but that doesn't mean that each is as comprehensive as it could be. Let's take a look at what a holistic master plan that takes both the day-to-day tasks as well as the future space use analyses into consideration.

Here's what a facility master plan in a hotel should include:

Zoning, regulation, covenant assessments

Space standards/benchmarks descriptions

Program of space use

Workflow analyses

Engineering assessment and plan

Block, fit, or stacking plans

Concept site plan or campus plan

Architectural image concepts

Long-term maintenance plan

Construction estimates

Phasing or sequencing plan (the sequence or projects)

Once a hotel facility manager does the proper footwork to make contact with all departments that influence their facility, they will be better equipped to support their organization as it makes profitable moves in the future.

Project Management for Streamlined Facilities

Because the name of the game for facility managers is safety, maintenance, and planning, it surely comes as no surprise to you that the manager must also develop and execute a laundry list of projects to ensure that everything on and in the building is running smoothly. Facility Management Equipment Log.

Here are some examples of how project management tactics can streamline a facility's overall efficiency:

The establishment of project schedules that include both scope and budgetary needs

Advising all workers, including employees and consultants, on development and work progress

Maintaining transparent databases on each and every project to ensure that higher-ups are advised of any changes to schedule, budget, or manpower in real time

The compiling of comprehensive training schedules to ensure that all employees are properly certified for any regulatory changes that may arise

Conducting budget estimates for all proposed construction projects

Coordinating any service or maintenance upgrades for the facility's systems

Conduct meetings and get approval for necessary space alterations which might be necessary for the modernization of the space

Developing internal audit processes to ensure that all applicable regulatory standards are met, including the new ISO 41001, Facility management – Management systems – Requirements with guidance for use

Hotel Facilities Demand Organization

Best Leadership Practices for Facility Managers

Facility management is a big, often complex job that requires a strong, forward-thinking, and most of all, responsible leader who thinks about their facility's needs in as holistic of a manner as possible. In addition to possessing these qualities, the most informed managers either have years of diverse industry experience under the belt or have earned a specialized degree in the discipline. Continuing education is also common in the field, and there are a number of facilities management courses that can help facility managers stay up-to-date on current trends and best practices.

Facility Management Role

So, now that we have an idea of what an adept facility manager might look like on paper, let's delve into the most effective leadership practices they can implement to guarantee the safety and efficiency of their organization:

They are on the same page as the higher-ups in regards to the future – As mentioned throughout this guide, being a powerful facility manager means looking ahead into the future. From compiling business continuity plans in the event of a disaster to keeping an open line of communication with other departments, the manager understands that they will only be a true leader if their facility and staff are ready to roll with the changes.

They know how to plan and budget – Facility managers know the current value of every part of their facility's infrastructure – and how much it will take to upgrade. They also have an acute understanding of how their budgetary needs might ebb and flow moving forward so that they can accurately propose budgetary changes to the powers that be.

They have a feel for developing a great team – Depending on the specific needs of the organization, the facility manager might be responsible for the hiring and training of the facility workers, contractors, or even consultants. This means that the manager needs to have an innate understanding of the duties and restraints of each position and how they can best work together to make the most capable team possible. Remember, these team members are ultimately in control of the safety and security of the facility, very important jobs that can break an organization in regards to liability if something were to go awry.

They are willing to listen – It's only natural for facility managers to become frustrated with higher-ups calling for big shifts who might be physically disconnected with the facility, but that doesn't mean that they are wrong. Dynamic leaders collaborate with all departments by listening to their propositions and ideas. By doing so, they create an open, safe line of communication that, no matter the outcome, will strengthen interdepartmental relations.

Hotel Facility management is a challenging job, and it's one that grows increasingly complex as technology advancements reshape old processes into newer, streamlined approaches. The best facility managers understand exactly how to balance smart technology investments that boost efficiency while minimizing risks (e.g., fiscal and safety risks) for a positive influence on the bottom line. In short, facility management is the backbone of operations across a multitude of industries today.

In business world, the perspectives of entrepreneurial Strategies are crucial for growth. Driven by this urge, the strategic management has modeled concepts and principles towards this managerial cause. In its approach, the strategy evaluates the business operational environment and focus on the inner working of a company. In this case, it develops methodological advances and ideas that follow and target at predicting the transformation of the management practice. This paper aims to examine the strategies of management employed by the Marriott Hotels executives. For example, The Marriott Hotels choose the 'generic' strategy.The differentiation Strategy is the 'generic' approach chosen by The Marriott Hotels to market it products in the highly competitive hotel industry. Marriot International is an enterprise that has successfully employed the business-level generic strategies. The business is a global franchise or and a lodging and hotel facilities entity. These products display the Marriott facility to be the one of the top players in the accommodation sector, and the phenomenon is projected to be stabilised for a number of future years. This projection is anchored on the various competitive advantages at the disposal of the company (Marriott International Brands 34). These advantages include cost, uniqueness, and their competitiveness extent. The Marriott Global Incorporation follows a variety of strategies at the entrepreneurial level. The plans are showcased by the Marriott's vast brand portfolio that enables them to command a strong market presence in the hospitality industry. This approach is part of the strategy for the entity persuinng differentiation. The Marriot Incorporation differentiation plan is factored in developing a service and product that satisfies, in a unique way, the need of its customer. The approach is affected by the provision of several options of lodging that ranges from average to premium priced packages. The secret of value-addition offered by the uniqueness of the firm warrant it to peg a higher premium charge for hotels in the upmarket.

The way through which Marriott Hotels is implementing its strategy of differentiation

For example, Marriott Hotels is implementing its strategy of differentiation by integrating its market segmentation strategies with its every operation step. The Marriott management immediately realized, from the beginning, that one brand of the whole hotel enterprise could not offer adequate catering to every need of the guests (Harmon 2). As a result, the hotel chain utilized an extensive strategy of differentiation by creating various hotel brands. Each of the product names offered services to varied clients in the hospitality market. In this strata, products range from the low-end to high-end services. The upscale offers comprise of such products as Marriott JW Resorts, Ritz Carlton and Spas that are packaged for customers who desire luxurious and high-end accommodations (Marriott International Brands 34). Others are the Marriott Courtyard with a designed in-room space offices for the business traveler. The Fairfield Inn product offers quality service for the budget travelers. This mix of a variety of brands ensures that the Marriott International meets and fulfills any desire of every consumer regardless of her or his purchasing power. In this segmentation, the JW Marriott, Ritz Carlton, Marriott Resorts, and Hotels are promoted towards the clients desiring more experience in upscale lodging. These customers also have a strong will to pay a relatively higher cost of an added luxurious amenity. The Marriott Courtyard segment offers the business travelers an office space set-up in their units where they may be productive after business trip hours. Springhill Suites segments is a hotel offering that is moderate for a family or a single traveler with living area for unwinding before embarking on a good rest at nights (Harmon 2). The Townplace Suites and Residence Inn give accommodations an extended stay for traveler's searching for a place that is more like home. These hostels encompass living areas, full-size kitchens and sleeping quarters. In addition, the hospitality chain has a budget traveler suite with accommodations of Marriott quality. In overall, the firm has as a Marriott for all form of occasions. These products and helps the chain in its noble mission of molding loyalty to its customers. As illustrated, through this segmentation Marriott Hotels has implemented its strategy of differentiation in a unique way.

Evaluation of the Marriott Hotels' current strategy in the light of the analysis

In my opinion, the market segmentation strategy used by the hotels is a proper approach to creating a wide base of consumer. There is success for the company in this strategy, especially by segmentation its market in threefold and allocating specific price to each brand. These three categories of products. For example, the company has substantially served the high-end market in the Marriott JW Resorts, Ritz Carlton, and Spas products that are packaged for customers who desire luxurious and high-end accommodations. In addition, The Marriott Courtyard segment offers the business travelers an office space set-up in their units where they may be productive after business trip hours (Harmon 2). Springhill Suites segments is a hotel offering that is moderate for a family or a single traveler with living area for unwinding before embarking on a good rest at nights. The Townplace Suites and Residence Inn give accommodations an extended stay for traveler is searching for a home-like place. As a result, every consumer need is properly and adequately catered for without compromise in the high-quality service pursued by the Marriott Hotels management.

In my opinion, the hotel has other strategies that it may exploit. These include the Franchising and the approach Cost Leadership in its marketing mix. In addition to the market segmentation, the company should try to strengthen each brand as per its category. In this case, the firm will be able to create a strong brand identity with its consumers at all its levels of the market. As a result, it will be able to capture the mass market for its products. The increased demand will enable the firm to move high volumes of products thereby increasing its turnovers. As a result, it will be able to design a proper pricing system, as high turnovers will have high-profit levels. In addition, the company may employ the franchising strategy. In this case, it will be able to forego its traditional direct control of its hotels especially in the economies overseas. As a result, it might now concentrate its crucial business (Harmon 2). Furthermore, it will win in substantially reduce the financial risk associated with enormous businesses while allowing a more non-participatory global growth. The company may use this opportunity of franchising, as many investors are willing to collaborate with it due to its strong Marriott brand. This strategy will offset the threat of stiff competition the company is facing from its rival as Hilton and other hotels.

● Hotel cost / expense control management strategy

For hotel owners looking to grow their business, a robust revenue management strategy is of the utmost importance, helping to optimise business results. However, under the broader revenue management umbrella, there are many smaller strategies that can help to facilitate growth. In this article, you find nine revenue management strategies that those in the hotel industry can employ to achieve this ultimate objective.

What is Revenue Management?

Revenue management is a popular concept within the hotel industry, and is used to optimise a hotel or resort's financial results by maximising revenue. The accepted definition is: selling the right hotel room, to the right customer, at the right time, for the right price, via the right channel, with the best cost efficiency.Typically, it requires businesses to make effective use of performance data and analytics to predict demand, establish a dynamic pricing model and maximise the amount of revenue that the company brings in. Although revenue management is applicable to other industries, it has significance in the hospitality industry because hotels deal with a perishable inventory, fixed costs and varied levels of demand. Revenue management is considered important because it takes the guesswork out of key pricing decisions. More extended information about revenue management you can read in the article "What is revenue management?".

Revenue Management Strategies

1. Understand Your Market

In order to implement a successful revenue management strategy, it is imperative that you have a clear understanding of your market, where demand comes from and the various different local factors that might affect seasonal demand. You also need to be aware of your audience and their needs, wants and expectations.

Learn From Our Expert Partners

Moreover, you need to understand the competition that exists within the market and make strategic decisions regarding price, discounts and advertising with this competition in mind. Remember, this competition may not always be obvious, and may not always be in the same location as your hotel.

2. Segmentation and Price Optimisation

The concept of selling the right room to the right person at the right price requires you to appropriately segment your customer base. To do this, you need to identify different 'types' of customer and then look at these different segments and evaluate when they book hotel rooms or hotel facilities, how they book them and other habits. When this is carried out, it allows you to optimise prices for those different segments. One of the key advantages of this is that once prices are optimised for a particular segment, price changes can be minimised. This, in turn, can help to generate customer loyalty from those who appreciate the price consistency you offer.

3. Work Closely With Other Departments

Next, it is important to achieve close collaboration between the various different hotel departments, such as sales and marketing, in order to ensure that your revenue management strategies and their individual departmental strategies are in alignment with one another, and so that you can address challenges collectively. Identify key departmental decision-makers and bring them on board. Work with them to make adjustments to your revenue management strategies, rather than imposing your will, which might be met with resistance. Close collaboration will also help to ensure that you are always presenting consistent messages to customers and clients.

4. Forecasting Strategies

One of the most important aspects of revenue management is forecasting, which allows you to anticipate future demand and revenue, enabling necessary adjustments to be made. Within the hospitality industry, high-quality forecasting relies on accurate records being kept, including occupancy, room rates and revenue. Most forecasting strategies rely heavily on using historical data to spot trends. For example, if you notice an upturn in business in the past three Julys, it is sensible to assume the same may occur next time. However, forecasting also requires an awareness of current bookings, competitors' performance, local events and wider industry trends.

5. Embrace Search Engine Optimisation

Search engines offer one of the single biggest opportunities for those operating in the hotel industry to attract customers, which makes search engine optimisation an important part of a robust revenue management strategy. Through SEO, hotel owners can improve the visibility of their website on search engine results pages. As a consequence, you can improve the chances of attracting business from customers who are not specifically searching for your hotel, but who are searching for a hotel in your location. To achieve this, it is best to operate a solid content marketing strategy, and ensure your website's design is optimised for SEO purposes.

6. Choose the Right Pricing Strategy

There are many different pricing strategies out there, and no one strategy will guarantee success. Instead, those in the hospitality sector need to consider the best strategy for their particular hotel, based on what they have to offer, who they are trying to attract and what strategy their competitors are employing. A competitive pricing strategy, where prices are set based on other hotels prices, puts your business in direct competition and is good when your hotel has more to offer than your rivals do. Yet, in slow seasons, a discount strategy might be best, because a low-paying customer is better than an empty room. Another option is the value-added approach, where rates are higher, but additional value is provided through extras and freebies.

7. Incentives For Direct Bookings

While it is certainly important to cater for all distribution channels and meet customers where they are, rather than where you want them to be, it is also sensible to try to maximise the number of direct bookings that are made. The primary reason for this is because direct bookings do not require the commission to be paid to third parties, which means they are ideal for maximising revenue. One option is to offer exclusive incentives, such as loyalty points, or freebies, for customers who book directly through your own website.

Increase Revenue by Outsourcing Revenue Management

Revenue management is a proven concept, based on the idea of using data and analytics to optimise financial results. It also requires specific skills and knowledge, which means that it can be more effective to outsource revenue management to a third party that specialises in this area.

8. Focus on Mobile Optimisation

For those in the hotel industry, mobile has become one of the single most important revenue streams. As a result, any hotel or resort that is operating without having prioritised mobile optimisation is already operating at a distinct disadvantage compared to their competitors. Make sure your website is optimised for mobile viewing, meaning it loads quickly, the pages display properly on mobile devices and all buttons are fully functional. In addition, you need to ensure your booking process is also optimised, so that customers can book rooms from their mobile device, without needing to switch to desktop.

9. Work With a Freelance Revenue Manager

Finally, in many cases it can be beneficial to enlist the help of a freelance revenue manager, who will be able to bring knowledge, expertise and experience into your organisation. Freelancers are used to coming into hotels and getting to work quickly, and can work as and when you need them. Appointing a full-time revenue manager internally means employing them full-time, but a freelancer will only need to be paid for the work they actually do, meaning less of their time will be wasted. Moreover, because of their established expertise, you will be able to save money on costs associated with training them.

The concept of selling the right hotel room, to the right customer, at the right moment, for the right price, via the right channel is important for maximising revenue and facilitating growth. By following the nine revenue management strategies above, owners in the hospitality industry can improve their chances of achieving this.–

● Hotel service management strategy

For hotels, successful marketing depends on addressing a number of key points. These include: what a company or an industry like a hotel is going to produce; how much a hotel is going to charge; how that particular hotel is going to deliver its products or services to the guests; and how it is going to tell its customers about its products and services. Traditionally, these considerations were known as the 4Ps of the hotel industry — Product, Price, Place, and

Promotion. As marketing became a more sophisticated discipline in the hospitality industry, a fifth 'P' was added and implemented— People. And recently, two further 'P's were added, mainly for service industries (like the hospitality industry)— Process and Physical evidence. These considerations are now known as the 7 Ps of service marketing in the hotel industry and sometimes referred to as the marketing mix of the hospitality industry!

In the realm of hotels, marketing is a technique of guiding the customers to choose your goods and service rather than electing the products of your rivals. If a hotel is not accounting for this aspect to make their brand more relevant, they are hampering their profit level, sales, and occupancy. The key for all hotels is to search the correct channel of marketing (which may be Display Advertising, Email Marketing, Pay-Per-Click Advertising (PPC) or Online Public Relations) and disclosing the accurate message in order to influence the targeted guests.

How to manage luxury hotel

The hotel industry has welcomed an unprecedented level of luxury. The rising demand for this extravagance is the increasing guest pursuit of meaningful, personalized experiences that are at the same time unique, exclusive and memorable. At luxury hotels, we work with a number of hotels that offer such services. From this first-hand experience, we have seen that luxury hotel guests don't want to be seen as capricious and wasteful. They value their privacy, yet seek out luxury stays for the unique surprises and thrills that hotel management can offer.However, it may have different kinds of service peformance strategies for luxury and not luxury hotel service perfomance, it may differ as below:

Outstanding Luxury Hotel Services hotel positioning strategy

1. Paparazzi Police

Keeping their vacation private is the minimum that your guests can ask of your luxury hotel, right? But, if for instance you have celebrity guests whose daily life involves being followed by paparazzi, maintaining such privacy presents challenges.To solve this paparazzi problem, for example the Las Ventanas hotel in Los Cabos, Mexico came up with an innovative solution to ensure their guests' privacy and an enjoyable stay. This hotel's staff are equipped with reflective screens, which protect their guests from prying photographers. These "Paparazzi Police" use their screens to shine light at the photographers, which ruins their photos.

2. Personalized Firework Display

We focus on Las Ventanas again, as the luxury hotel offers a spectacular personalized, private fireworks show. Costing around $1,700 per minute, guests can easily personalize it to their liking. It is another service that helps create a truly unique, unforgettable experience in a part of the world that is known for its mesmerizing natural beauty.

3. Hot Air Balloon Ride

Breathtaking experiences are a favorite of luxury hotel guests prepared to pay extra for the privilege. One such experience is a ride in a hot air balloon. And one such hotel that offers this service is the Kale Konak Hotel, located atop Cappadocia in Turkey. Leveraging its position amid a location of natural splendor, this hotel helps its guests by organizing a hot air balloon ride, which promises a stunning experience of a lifetime.

How can your hotel take advantage of its surroundings to offer thrilling adventures and experiences?

4. Sunscreen-Spraying Booths

Hotel guests don't want to worry about anything when they enjoy the beach or the resort pool at remote and exclusive locations. And if there's one thing that can ruin a vacation, it's sunburn. Proactive hotels take it upon themselves to help guests prevent burning up by including sunscreen-spraying booths as a standard luxury hotel service. In particular, many Caribbean hotels offer this service, loved by solo travelers, couples and families alike. After all, even if a guest carelessly forgets to apply sunscreen and suffers the consequences, they are much more likely to associate your hotel with the negative experience. By offering sunscreen-spraying booths, you cancel out this possibility and create a value-added service for your guests, so they can enjoy their vacation in full.

5. Sunscreen-Spraying Booth

For hotels that are located with expansive countryside hills nearby, paragliding is a luxury service that ticks all the boxes. It can be relatively inexpensive to run, offers a riveting add-on experience, and will hep move you head and shoulders above your competition. A novel twist is to offer a paragliding route from atop a hill to the hotel entrance at the bottom. With the help of a professional paragliding expert, the most demanding and fearless of guests can enjoy an extreme sport and make a rock-star entrance at your hotel.

6. Secret, Invite-Only Room

It is an increasing trend to offer a secret or hidden service. But the catch is that it can't be bought by money. Certain luxury desires can only be attained with the right contact, recommendation, knowledge or invite. Think of the appeal of speakeasy bars, or exclusive, secret societies. Take advantage of this winning trend by creating a secret, invite-only room in your hotel. Make it exceptionally beautiful or intriguing, or offer services that are unobtainable to "regular" guests. Choose a secluded or forbidden area of your hotel for its location. And of course, this secret room cannot be advertised on your official channels, such as your website.

7. In-Suite Shopping

Luxury is never having to pack a suitcase, no matter where you go or for how long. Take inspiration from London's Hotel Café Royal, which offers its guests a personalized, curated styling service for all occasions during their stay. Guests check in without luggage and find a selection of clothes handpicked by a personal stylist to choose from in their suite upon arrival. By offering your guests this luxury option, you make them feel like pop stars. And not only is it extremely convenient, everyone loves discovering a new outfit to wear and feeling like a VIP.

8. Complimentary Luxury Car Drives

Some of the very best 5-star luxury hotels offer their guests luxury cars during their stay too, for free. Hotels like The Peninsula Beverly Hills in California provide their guests with Rolls-Royce and Infiniti cars, having developed a strong relationship with the high-end car manufacturers. If you have the budget to ramp up your luxury hotel with this complimentary service, it will help serve as a magnet for guests eager for exclusive experiential stays. And if not, there are other options. For instance, you can approach high-end car leasing companies to enquire about reaching an agreement. And it doesn't have to be luxury cars. You could also tap into the growing importance of sustainability to guests by offering premium eco-friendly cars.

9. No-Internet Digital Detox Zone

C-suite executives and stressed millionaires with companies and scores of people dependent on their decisions and attention find it difficult if not impossible to disconnect. With so much responsibility on their shoulders, they are often available around the clock, seven days a week. Even if they do get an opportunity to get some much needed time off, they are often interrupted by a colleague who needs their input on the latest emergency or major decision at their company. Cue the growing prevalence of no-internet resorts. No WiFi, no mobile internet signal and no onsite computers to access the web. Completely and utterly offline.

This digital detox is increasingly sought after by hyper-connected individuals who want to get away from it all, even if only for a few days, offering them total peace and quiet, without the fear of their phone blowing up with calls, messages and emails. For typically busy company executives and such individuals in an ultra-connected world, this kind of opportunity to unwind and relax "off the grid" is an increasingly exclusive luxury.

On conclusion, more and more hotels are trying to make their guests' stay as special as possible so in the near future, many of these unconventional services will be offered by more luxurious hotels all over the world. This being said, a great hotel manager goes beyond what customers say they want, helping them to realize their wildest dreams by combining fun, joyful experiences with exclusive, unique services that make them feel important.

For hotels, successful marketing depends on addressing a number of key points. These include: what a company or an industry like a hotel is going to produce; how much a hotel is going to charge; how that particular hotel is going to deliver its products or services to the guests; and how it is going to tell its customers about its products and services. Traditionally, these considerations were known as the 4Ps of the hotel industry — Product, Price, Place, and Promotion. As marketing became a more sophisticated discipline in the hospitality industry, a fifth 'P' was added and implemented— People. And recently, two further 'P's were added, mainly for service industries (like the hospitality industry)— Process and Physical evidence. These considerations are now known as the 7 Ps of service marketing in the hotel industry and sometimes referred to as the marketing mix of the hospitality industry!

Hence, in the realm of hotels, marketing is a technique of guiding the customers to choose your goods and service rather than electing the products of your rivals. If a hotel is not accounting for this aspect to make their brand more relevant, they are hampering their profit level, sales, and occupancy. The key for all hotels is to search the correct channel of marketing (which may be Display Advertising, Email Marketing, Pay-Per-Click Advertising (PPC) or Online Public Relations) and disclosing the accurate message in order to influence the targeted guests.

Before providing an excellent service is experienced, it first has to be delivered. It, therefore, means that the process of choosing to use a service might be perceived as risky since one is buying something that is intangible. To reduce this uncertainty, physical evidence such as case studies should be used. This can be done by keeping the facilities clean, well decorated and tidy. The physical evidence that is demonstrated by an organization should be able to confirm the assertions of the customers. Although it might not be possible for the customers to experience the service before they have purchased, the customers can talk to other customers with experience!

GUEST ENGAGEMENT GUEST EXPERIENCE HOTEL INDUSTRY HOTEL MARKETING HOTEL REVENUE MANAGEMENT MARKETING

Hotel-sales-strategies-direct-bookings

Your worst nightmare as a hotelier is walking down the halls of your hotel and realising that rooms are empty. There's a sad stillness that not only marks the sign of a quiet moment, but also the sign of a failing business strategy. In order to avoid this situation at any point during the year – even during the slow travel season – you need to implement sales strategies that will improve business and continually bring in more guests. The first, and most obvious reason, to focus on increasing hotel room sales is because this will drive revenue. With additional revenue on-hand, you are able to provide guests with the service they expect, as well as move the hotel forward into the future. Before you can dabble in additional packages, add-on excursions and luxury upgrades, you must be able to sell rooms. Another reason to prioritise hotel room sales techniques is to provide guests with the atmosphere that they expect. A vacant or nearly empty hotel is not a good look to people who are staying there. You want to be able to sell as many rooms as possible so that you can provide your guests with a lively, charismatic environment.

- Essential hotel room sales strategies

Every hotelier needs to implement sales strategies that work best for their own target market as well as for their local destination. Ultimately, it is up to the hotel operator or manager to create a customised sales strategy that will drive the most room sales at their own individual property, but these are some of the top hotel room sales strategies to consider:

1. Hotel group sales strategy

This strategy may require an overhaul of your normal marketing and sales approach. The idea is to sell rooms and meeting spaces to corporate groups; it's important you can offer a deal for both. Landing these types of sales requires innovation but it can be very beneficial for repeat business if you do. The most cost effective way to secure group bookings is by connecting directly to planners. You can list your property on venue marketplaces where planners can view floorplans, photos, and unique differentiators. It's also important to segment your target audience so you can make compelling offers to the right kind of groups for your property.

2. Hotel direct sales strategy

With this sales strategy, the priority is to earn direct bookings online from as many guests as possible. Direct bookings are the most beneficial booking for hotel operators because these bookings generate the most revenue. There are no agents or other distribution partners that must be paid a commission when a guest books directly online. In order to implement a direct booking strategy, hotel managers should invest in an online booking system that syncs with their existing website and property management system. Hotel operators should also prioritise their social media strategy when focusing on increasing direct bookings.

3. Destination marketing sales strategy

This type of sales strategy requires a hotel operator to work with other tourism business professionals in their destination to promote the region as a whole. Through a destination marketing campaign, local businesses team up to target the most powerful inbound tourism markets and drive more traffic to the general area.

4. Cross-promotional sales strategy

With this sales strategy, hotel managers need to identify and evaluate various large events that will be taking place in the local region throughout the calendar year. Then, the hotel operator needs to come up with a promotion that can coincide with the event, ultimately allowing them to earn an influx of bookings that they may not otherwise have had. Opportunities that are ideal for a cross-promotional sales strategy include an upcoming industry conference, a concert or a major sporting event.

5. Guest rewards sales strategy

Many travellers today, particularly the powerful millennial generation, value the opportunity to earn rewards with the companies that they do business with. Hotels, in particular, have great success with rewards programs. In a guest rewards sales strategy, the manager or operator should develop a system that rewards guests for staying frequently, for purchasing upgrades, and for referring friends and family members. A rewards sales strategy often generates repeat bookings, which are particularly lucrative for hotel operators.

6. Revenue management sales strategy

This type of sales strategy aims to maximise the number of rooms booked at any point in the year, regardless of the typical travel traffic at that particular point in time. Typically, a revenue management plan requires hotel operators to drop room rates during the low season in order to encourage bookings, while raising rates during high traffic times. During these moments, guests are going to be willing to pay higher rates to get a room, so it's worthwhile raising rates to generate more revenue per available room.

Other room selling techniques in hotels

Large, overarching, strategies are vital to drive a consistent level of business at your hotel but there are other smaller tactics you can use to sell your rooms or generate more revenue from each guest:

Upselling – Upselling is the process of selling a more expensive version of the service or product your customer is buying. The methods you use to upsell need to be handled with a degree of delicacy. The timing, tone, and regularity with which you upsell is the key to the success of your efforts. You don't want to seem pushy so treat it as an exercise in awareness rather than a sales pitch. Make sure guests know what options are available to them but let them initiate any further interest.

Re-marketing – Re-marketing allows you to reach out to potential guests who have visited your site without finalising their booking. Many travellers will visit a variety of different websites to explore their options during the research phase of their online booking journey. With re-marketing strategies, you can access these customers again at different points during their online booking experience and remind them to visit your site again to book with you.

Incentives or cross-selling – Cross-selling is the process of selling an additional, supplementary product or service to complement the product or service your customer is buying. Offering incentives in the form of additional products or services may just be the thing that gets your guest to confirm a booking. Think added-value items like a free massage, or a local tour.

Build local partnerships – Unless your hotel is located in a remote or isolated destination, there should be plenty of other businesses and attractions you can form a mutually beneficial partnership with. Co-promoting with restaurants, specialty shops like ski hire, adventure companies, theme parks, or museums can help lead to easy and effective marketing. And these kind of partnerships can work no matter how the guest is planning their trip – be it to book accommodation first, or create their itinerary before looking for a hotel.

Make booking easy on your website – The importance of a good website experience for travellers can't be overstated. Nothing will drain their excitement quicker than a slow, confusing, or convoluted website. Make sure yours is clean, intuitive, mobile-friendly, and has clear action buttons such as 'book now' for potential guests to click. When direct bookings are so valuable, your website has to be a priority.

● Hotel promotion strategy

Promotions are great because you can be very flexible and targeted with what you offer, and often they'll grab the attention of travellers searching online. This is where it can actually be useful to steer into what guests might expect, such as promotions around seasons, themes, events, direct, bookings, or partnerships.

1. Seasonal promotions

Most destinations experience a low season, where tourism is not as active as other parts of the year. However, with the right deals your hotel doesn't have to suffer through empty rooms and hallways. Try to incorporate discounts with eye-catching promotions like 'Summer Getaways' and 'Winter Retreats' and remind travellers how beautiful your destination is and how much they can see when there are less crowds.

2. Themed promotions

These will be attention-grabbing and very relevant for travellers looking into booking a stay in the area. For example you might offer promotions around honeymoons or anniversaries if you're in a romantic locale, adventure deals if you're out of the major cities, or ultimate relaxation experiences if you're a coastal hotel. Appealing to different lifestyles or family setups is always a good idea.

3. Event-based promotions

It makes a lot of sense to capitalise on events and include them in your promotions. People will already be researching these events so if your hotel has a deal on in conjunction with them, awareness of your hotel should increase along with site traffic. These events might include music or art festivals, Easter or Christmas events, circuses, travelling markets, sporting events etc. With a booking you might offer discounted tickets, adapt the hotel experience to match the events, create special rates.

4. Direct booking promotions

Placing exclusive promotions within your booking engine on your website will give travellers an incentive to book direct instead of via an OTA. It will also help establish your hotel website as your most important distribution channel and help increase profit by eliminating OTA commission fees. The incentive might be a discount, or it might also be an added extra such as a bottle of wine, restaurant voucher, or amenity gift cards.

5. Partnership promotions

Combining with other businesses will reduce the cost of promotion and marketing, and give you wider coverage as long as your partner holds up their end of the bargain. It may also give you access to a new market and create ongoing business. Common partnerships include those with theme parks, restaurants, cinemas, museums, sporting arenas, adventure and tour guides. It's one thing to create your promotions, but remember you need people to see them. Always advertise on your social media channels and ensure your search engine optimisation is strong

6. Mobile-only promotions

Year on year, nearly every statistic points to an upsurge of mobile usage on hotel, travel, and booking websites, with projected numbers even more prominent. As quick as online booking overtook more traditional and outdated methods, mobile is starting to usurp desktop. Implementing smart and effective mobile strategies will boost customer experience and keep your hotel competitive within an industry that never stops innovating.

● Hotel packages strategy

Use other businesses to enrich your packages – Combining your services with that of another tourist attraction in the area is a surefire way to add value to your packages. It also gives you a lot of flexibility on what you can offer guests. Tickets to zoos, tours, theme parks, museums are always popular as are restaurant vouchers. Even concerts or one-off events can be leveraged as short-term packages. This way you can cater for many different guests, those interested in adventure and those more excited by shopping or fine dining.

Promote one-stop shopping – Savvy travellers will look at your packages and wonder exactly what kind of deal they're getting. Unless you and your business partner agree to offer discounted prices it's likely the combined price of a room and a tour package will be similar to the components purchased separately. This is why you need to advertise the convenience and quality of what you're offering, rather than spruiking the cost.

Be creative with your choices – Guests might become rather bored if they see yet another 'romance' package. Try incorporating more interesting content into your packages and their names. For instance a 'bucket list' package might include a selection of passes or discounts to the absolute must-sees of the local area. This will be an attractive option for guests because it's likely they already interested in visiting those landmarks. For business travellers, always focus on convenience such as a package delivering breakfast to their room, free dry cleaning, and transport services.

Use your own property to add value – While most packages include a room and some type of external activity, you can make your packages even more enticing by adding your own service to the mix such as spa-treatments or a bar tab. Guests will want to experience your amenities and they'll be more likely to pay to do so if it's included in a package.

Cater for speciality markets – Never ignore families. Often it's the children you're appealing to most because parents will be looking for activities that will occupy the kids. The same principle applies if you're a pet-friendly hotel. You must also consider guests with disabilities and people with specific occupations that you can give personalised packages to. Don't forget to promote any new packages you create, be they long-term or one-off. Use Facebook, Twitter, Instagram, and your email sends to drum up business. Send any information along to your local tourism office so they can do the same. Another thing to consider is what you want to achieve with your packages. Sometimes they can create a lot of brand awareness, even if they don't attract much business directly.

direct-sales-hotel

To the average traveller you and your competitors will often appear very similar. That's why you need to present an offer that tips the balance and convinces an undecided traveller yours is the best hotel for them. Package deals and extras are an easy, but extremely effective way of doing this, providing you take the right approach.

Your hotel distribution strategy and how it impacts sales

Implementing a successful sales strategy requires you to have an effective distribution strategy. Hotel operators must network with industry professionals as well as agents to sell their rooms to the maximum number of people in a variety of target market segments. Common agents that are included in any distribution strategy include retail travel agents, visitor information centres, local businesses, online travel agents, and destination marketing organisations. Hotel operators and managers must recognise that their distribution network is a fluid, living entity, and they should constantly be looking for new and innovative ways to reach out to new agents and distributors.

In addition to expanding and developing a diverse distribution network, hotel operators must be able to effectively distribute their rooms to all of their agents in real-time. The only way to do this is to partner with a channel manager that connects to your property management system. With a channel manager, hotel operators can provide their live availability to every distribution agent that they have, regardless of their location or time zone. This allows them to sell as many rooms as possible — including securing those valuable last-minute bookings. It also significantly reduces the risk of overbooking rooms at the property, particularly during high-volume times. A channel manager is necessary to implement any sales strategy that a manager wishes to employ at their individual property.

Hotel sales tools

Your hotel sales tools include anything that enable you to bring a guest into your hotel. This might mean your social media accounts, your email marketing campaigns, the phone on your front desk, guest feedback, or back-end hotel technology solutions.Though when you think of tools as objects or functional pieces of software you might consider these to help inform your sales strategy:

Social networks
Analytics tools such as Google
Survey tools
Online travel agents
Property management tools
Booking engines
Channel managers
Website builders

Identifying and using the right tools will depend on your property and the guests you want to attract but for the most part all properties need the same tools. The difference comes in how you use them. Data is extremely important so using tools that can give you detailed reporting functions is a great step to take. With enough data at your disposal, you can make informed decisions about how you sell, gaining an edge over any competitors who are following a 'cookie-cutter' approach. Obviously you need to be smart about you use the budget at your hotel and look at tools which will make life easier while helping deliver more revenue to the business.

Hotel sales software

When you think of sales software in a hotel context, it's better to think distribution software. Three key pieces of technology that could help you are a channel manager, online booking engine, and website builder. While they may not be strictly thought of as sales software, they are the key to driving sales and revenue in the hotel industry.

Channel manager

This is one of your greatest allies when distributing your rooms because it's a tool that manages all the different online travel agents (OTAs) you sell your rooms through, such as Booking.com, Expedia or Airbnb. The main operating principle is called "pooled inventory" which means updates to rates and availability are made automatically across all connected channels whenever and wherever a booking is made. Enabling a more effective way to promote your rooms will naturally create an increase in sales. Read our guide on channel managers to learn more.

Booking engine

Also a reservation system, this will secure online bookings from direct channels such as your own website and social media pages like Facebook. An online booking engine has become essential, especially with the rise of social media. Creating a friction-less experience for guests when they book direct will boost your conversion and improve your sales results. Read our guide on booking engines to learn more.

Website builder

This takes away the need for you to hire a web designer. Instead you can use this software to create a beautiful, search engine optimised, guest converting website in minutes. You simply have to provide your content and choose from a number of available templates. Your website is a major selling point for travellers – winning them over with an amazing first impression is imperative. With the right technology in place, you will be able to easily and effectively implement your hotel room sales strategies. To learn more about these hotel sales tools and to find out if they are the right choice for your hotel property, check out how they work in a video demo.

What to expect from these hotel room sales strategies ? When you sell hotel rooms, you do more than just get another guest in the door of your property. You are able to improve your hotel business in its entirety. Here are a few of the benefits that you will realise when you employ hotel room sales strategies that are designed to increase hotel room sales:

You will generate more revenue consistently throughout the entire year. An effective hotel sales strategy allows you to earn as much revenue as possible, regardless of the seasonal ebbs and flows of the tourism industry. You will be able to make improvements to your property. As you begin to earn more revenue from your bookings, you can make improvements that will generate buzz about your brand and continue to sell more rooms. Finally, you will be able to move beyond standard sales strategies and begin creating packages that increase the revenue you generate per guest. Once your sales steadily increase, you can begin to expand your offerings. Romance packages, adventure packages and luxury upgrades allow you to sell more rooms while also boosting the revenue you earn per booking.

● Hotel revenue management technology

What is revenue management for the hospitality industry? Revenue management refers to the strategic distribution and pricing tactics you use to sell your property's perishable inventory to the right guests at the right time, to boost revenue growth. Other products such as your amenities and food and beverage offerings will also come into the picture. Revenue management revolves around measurement of what customers from different segments are willing to pay, and this can only be done by measuring and monitoring the supply and demand of your hotel rooms.

Every traveller has a maximum value they can offer your hotel; revenue management is about capturing as much of this value as you possibly can. Preferably you'll do this by convincing the guest to book direct, purchase extensions, up-sells or extras, and become a return visitor. The best strategies are based on the understanding that hotel pricing is fluid, and can change from one day to the next. This is why you should never be afraid to increase your rates. Customers actually expect increases over time – most businesses where consumers spend money are varying their prices based on demand and shifts in costs.

Effective hotel revenue management strategies can also help hoteliers:

Better manage resources

Protect against rostering too many staff during slow periods

Ensure adequate numbers of staff are working during the busiest times

With all this in mind, revenue management can drive the entire business plan when implemented effectively. Your hotel distribution strategy is also a vital part of your revenue management plan. Make sure you are on the internet distribution channels that promote your destination online. They have strong marketing power and can put your hotel in front of many customers you can't contact directly.

How to increase hotel revenue ? Many strategies come into play when driving more revenue to your hotel, and many of them don't involve raising prices or playing with your rates much at all. Not least of these is satisfying your customer. If the product you offer is universally recognised as quality, you have the grounding to charge a higher price. If guests feel like they are getting maximum value for their money, it's very likely they'll be willing to spend more. Getting more out each individual guest who stays with you is a great way to increase the overall revenue of your hotel. For instance, guaranteed revenue from a guest you convince to stay an extra night by discounting the additional night might be worth your while, especially in low season.

A list of general tactics you can use to improve your hotel's revenue stream:

Be bookable online

These days travellers enjoy the flexibility, convenience, and value of booking online. By connecting to online travel agents/more online travel agents you'll easily see an uplift.

Build a revenue culture

Who's on your revenue team? Everyone! Anticipatory service + proactive revenue-minded employee = emotionally connected customer with engaged loyalty and higher revenue returns.

Sell other hotel products

Revenue opportunities extend far beyond simply selling your rooms. Think about the amenities you have on site and what your are charging for them, and go even further by offering hotel guests the chance to purchase items like soap, utensils, towels etc – especially if your hotel has a unique sense of style.

Leverage events and attractions

Local events and attractions are a great opportunity to put together packages for guests or offer additional services such as transport. The benefits are two-fold – guests will enjoy their stay more and your hotel will generate more income.

As you move away from tactics and towards fully fledged strategies around your revenue and room sales, you need to start understanding your key performance indicators (KPIs). Once you know what you should be looking at you can start analysing the data and developing ways to manipulate them in your favour.

As an introduction, these are the metrics you can explore:

Occupancy rate

ADR (Average daily rate)

RevPAR (Revenue per available room)

TrevPAR (RevPAR + ancillaries)

GOPPAR (Gross operating profit per available room)

RevPASH (Revenue per available seat hour) – useful if you have a hotel restaurant

The principle that you should always keep in mind is to assess market conditions in real-time and adapt accordingly.

Revenue management strategies

You need a revenue management strategy to remain sustainable – that's the short story. Ideally, you'll even be able to turn a tidy profit each year. The best hotel revenue management strategies recognise that hotel pricing is fluid, and can change from one day to the next. It's critical that any hotelier creates a revenue management strategy that is adaptable to the current conditions. Often it's more important to focus on your own business and be confident than to worry too much about competitors, at least at first.

Every hospitality business strategy has to have the customer at its heart. How do travellers behave in the current landscape? How do they book and travel? How do they experience and explore? What do they require? What are their expectations? It's vital you have an idea of these factors if you want to squeeze the most value out of each guest that enters your door. The better you know the guest the more guest loyalty you can generate, which is extremely important for recurring revenue. If you know you have a certain amount of guests returning each year, that's more rooms you don't have to worry about and you can focus more on upselling and cross-selling.

Hotel pricing strategies

There's no pricing strategy that is perfect for any hotel. Each property must consider the pricing strategy, or strategies, that work best for its particular brand. A revenue manager will spend a lot of time analysing data and other influencing factors to ensure the business is operating with the best possible chance to maximise income.

There are a number of questions that should surround your pricing strategies:

What do your guests want?

Which strategy will complement the business mix?

How will different strategies affect connected channels and distribution partners?

How does your strategy integrate with your channels?

Who are the experts that can help determine the right strategy?

With all that in mind, the first priority of pricing should be forecasting. This way you can predict demand so you can get travellers to book early. Then you can raise rates later as availability drops and demand increases. (This is an ideal pricing structure known as the "ascending model" whereby pricing increases closer to an arrival day.) We'll talk more about forecasting and analysis later.

What is dynamic pricing?

Dynamic pricing involves changing room rates daily or even within the day based on real-time market data. Taking supply and demand into account, prices should fluctuate regularly if you want to maximise revenue. This pricing option is well suited in today's market and is one many hoteliers opt to use.

Dynamic pricing examples

Put simply, there will be days where supply and demand will be very different depending on the time of day. In the morning you may have lower rates because your occupancy is low, as is demand. However by that evening supply may have reduced and demand grown. Many factors can drive this, such as competitors putting up their no vacancy signs or setting rates slightly too high, or travellers arriving late for events the next day and so on. You can raise your rates to take advantage of the shifting market and earn more revenue than if you'd kept your rates static.

What is open pricing?

Open pricing defines the flexibility hotels around the globe have to set their prices at different levels depending on the various target markets and distribution channels they deal with.

This luxury of choice allows hotels to forecast more accurately. For example, a high-end hotel may usually attract guests who no budget constraints but in the off-season bookings will drops and the hotel can drop rates to attract travellers who normally would not be able to afford the stay. While the average daily rate of the hotel will be lower, occupancy will remain steady and revenue will continue to turnover.

Other hotel pricing strategies

There are numerous pricing strategies you can use at your hotel as part of your broader revenue management strategy, many of them in conjunction. Here's a list of the most common pricing strategies your hotel might find useful:

1. Value-added pricing

You can set your room rates higher than the local competition while also offering more extras in the basic package. This gives the illusion that the hotel offers a premium experience that focuses on value rather than just low rates.

2. Discount pricing
Used in slow seasons to boost occupancy by dropping base rates. Revenue can be made up through other services in the hotel.
3. Price per segment
Offering the same product at different prices to different types of customers. E.g 'family rate'
Length of stay
When demand outweighs supply, it can help to implement a rule where guests are 'obligated' to stay a minimum number of days. In such cases, lower rates may not be necessary.
4. Positional pricing
Basing your rates off brand strength and reputation.
5. Penetration pricing
Positioning yourself as the cheapest in the market. Be mindful of how travellers will perceive your hotel – you need to retain the opportunity to sell at higher rates.
6. Skimming
Positioning your hotel among the most expensive. Price leaders often achieve among the highest profitability, however the consumers need to clearly understand the reasons that they would pay more for staying at your hotel.

What does hotel market segmentation mean?
Segmenting is a key aspect of revenue management. It allows you to differentiate between the travellers who are coming to your hotel and devise uniques strategies for all of them. For example, the approach you take with young adventurers will be very different to a business professional. However segmentation is more complex than simply business vs leisure, and you can use it to discover trends within your hotel business.
One of the best ways to identify and filter segments is by their reason for travel. Think family holiday, wedding, tourist event, adventure, relaxation, business, etc. However, more and more hotels are adopting a different strategy and defining market segment by how a reservation was made, e.g. Expedia as a market segment. This is known as "blended segmentation" – combining the reason for stay and method of booking. Hotel chains have adopted different applications of this traditional definition of a market segment and channels. Some hotel chains and groups identify a channel as an OTA, and then identify the likes of Booking.com's reward program and Expedia's Egencia (for corporate travel) as sub-channels.

Further segmentation factors that you should take into account include:

Length of stay
Days of the week of stays
Lead time (how long before arrival do they book)
Cancellations
No show ratio

Once you have a good grip on market segments you can start to decide which groups your business wants to focus on more, and which to close out at different times of the year. By drilling down further you might realise certain segments have higher cancellation rates and you could want to resist marketing to them. Each segment will have a unique opportunity for you to gain extra business or revenue.

Here's a quick snapshot of the possibilities:

Loyalty or rewards members – Offer discounts

Mobile booking – Use mobile exclusive promotions

Direct bookings – Make offers that only exist on your website

Walk-ins – Entice extra spending with your amenities

Corporate – A chance to negotiate rates with large companies

Online travel agents – Advertise special event packages

Groups – Combine with tour operators and attractions

Every piece of analysis you do helps you build the optimal business mix for your hotel, so it's important to look at all your options. If selling is a problem, there's always a new way to sell or new market to target. If spending is the problem, there's always a way to entice customers to open their wallets again.

Hotel price forecasting

Forecasting is not only important for rate setting, but also for budgeting purposes. Accurate and effective forecasting requires a strong foundation in historical data. By budgeting and forecasting in advance you'll have plenty of time and opportunity to make strategy adjustments. If you know one point in the year is particularly valuable to your hotel, write your forecast immediately for that period a year in advance. For example, try writing your December 2021 forecast on January 1st 2020.

Key components of an effective forecast include:

Occupancy

Revenue

Room rates

Turnaways/Regrets/Denials – tracking of reservations that are turned away or not booked, and is a critical measurement of demand. Ideally your turnaways are captured and measured on your online as well as direct/ telephone requests.

Spend per room

Reservations

Market trends

Hotel budgeting and demand forecasting

It's a good idea to create demand calendar prior to setting your budgeting plan so you know exactly what you're dealing with. Most hotels forecast every day for next 30 days and every week for next 90 days. A lot of hoteliers do this in a spreadsheet after extracting data from their PMS, but this is where you need really cool tech – and a really easy system – that can do it all in one place.

Take into account factors from last year and also the upcoming year. Mark the following as things to track:

RevPAR last year
Groups or events last year
Demand level indicator last year (High, Medium, Low, Distressed)
Public/bank holidays
School holidays
Indications of increased demand

This will allow you to make informed pricing strategies based on solid data sets.

Before you reach your ideal budget you have to take into account influences such as sales resources, online marketing and distribution, refurbishment needs, and developments your competitor set is making. Your budget should be developed on the basis of this question: at which rate and how many rooms can you sell for every future day? For example, how do you anticipate the business demand and the leisure demand per country? At which rate can you sell on the upcoming months? How will your main corporate accounts behave?

Two distinct demand measurements are constrained demand and unconstrained demand.

1. Constrained demand

Maximum demand for amount of rooms (the maximum number of bookings you could get based on the number of rooms) limited by the physical inventory.

2. Unconstrained demand

Maximum bookings you could get with unlimited rooms based on demand and not limited by the actual physical inventory.

You should identify when unconstrained demand is above the capacity of the hotel. This is an important part of your hotel revenue management strategy. The unconstrained demand will help you calculate your Last Room Value for certain dates, and possible length of stay restrictions that may apply.

Hotel benchmarking

Hotels will commonly benchmark against their competition to evaluate performance. It's not the definitive way to track performance, nor should it be treated as an authority, but it does enable you to see where you stand and how travellers might react.

You'll be required to benchmark on criteria such as:

Prices
Product (luxury, mid-range, economy?)
Level of service
Location
Distribution channel

Remember a competitor is only a competitor if they're targeting the same markets as you, and even then you might not be competing for the same segments at the same time. However, if you can anticipate their strategies, making your own adjustments will become much easier. In the context of the competitor set, results can often look very different. Perhaps you thought you only had an average year when in fact your competitors were much worse off and you were the stellar hotel in the area. Or vice versa.

On conclusion, hotel price control/income management strategy may bring below these benefits to any hotels as below, they may include as below:

1. Less costly errors

While larger hotels might be able to hide or easily overcome a pricing mistake, smaller hotels have less margin for error. An incorrect price at a small hotel will have a bigger impact on ADR and RevPAR.

2. Get more revenue out of every room

With fewer rooms, maximising the rate for each room becomes more critical. The data your technology provides will help you understand who you should be targeting and when. What will be the most valuable demand for you? For example, do you offer rates for group business? Do you offer discounts for long stays?

3. Know your competitors better

To get your own pricing strategy right, you need to know what your immediate competitors are doing. With a pricing intelligence tool you can get an instant all-in-one overview of your competitors rate activity, meaning you can concentrate on why they are adjusting and how/if you should respond.

4. It makes your hotel 'bigger'

Large, branded hotels will already have an RMS in place – and dedicated revenue managers to manage them – and while independent hotels may not be able to afford a robust solution, pricing intelligence tools are an affordable substitute. These use the data and its own algorithms to carry out a real-time analysis of the state of the market, and of demand, in order to calculate ideal room rates. Increasing your data visibility and analysis capabilities gives you more ammunition to compete with large hotel groups who are able to devote full-time staff to revenue management.

5. Manage your time efficiently

Automated market intelligence will allow you to instantly access and act upon pricing data. Knowing when the market will be an easy sell-out or in a quiet period will not only enable you to optimise rates, but with a dependable forecast, you can organise your staff more effectively and improve the guest experience.

6. You can be proactive

The more data you have access to, the less reactive you'll be. Rather than reacting to your competitors all the time, you'll better understand demand, make your own projections, and set intelligent rates.

7. Understand your guests better

A RMS can tell you more about customer behaviour and allow you to attract more bookings. For example, do guests prefer it when your rate applies to every night of their stay, or will they accept varying rates, or do they prefer a total stay price?

8. Your data will come from a single source

Instead of combing through your own data, and then individually doing the same for competitors, an RMS will collate everything for you in one place. Depending on your system, you can do this for up to 15 competitors. If you are a smaller hotel that is new to revenue management strategies, doing everything manually might have you tearing your hair out. Hence, any hotels can not neglect to consider how to implement price and income management strategy in order to achieve the highest profit aim.

Q2 Can Airlines fuel manufacturing supply strategy reduce operational cost ?

However, there are some airlines which are the characteristic of self organization . It means that they are present in that both of oil fuel production and providing flights service in airline industry. So, these self organization airlines can control the oil fuel price by themselves. However, any self supply airline organization is also evident in efforts by businesses acts of terrorism against economic targets by adopting proactive steps, such as airline and airport security. So, it seems any self suply airline organization can reduce the risk to avoid oil price raising and terrorism attacks in airline industry risk management sector because oil shortage won't influence their air ticket prices need to be raised. Beside, these self supply airline organizations which have high technology of fuel efficient aircrafts, the use of one aircraft model, the adoption of direct routes versus customer loyalty programs and other operational cost reductions are strategies for increased profitability.

To solve oil price, terrorism etc. external risk to airline industry. Instead of high technology of fuel efficient aircrafts and self supply airline organization methods can solve terrorism attacks and oil price rising risks. However, I believe that there are other risks will threaten to airline industry. This risks concern traveller individual psychological factors influence, so it means that any airlines can apply psychological methods to predict which airline passengers' travel consumption desires. The risks include such as (1) user factor, such as : the travel country culture and tradition difference will influence the traveler chooses to prefer to go to the country to travel , the traveler's education level is high , who will choose to go to developed countries to travel, e.g. USA, UK. Otherwise, if the traveler's education level is low, who will choose to go to developing countries to travel, e.g. China, India etc. (2) economic factor, such as air tickets and airline fuel costs, (3) human resources and macro economic factor, such as political stability, economic development, educational policy, health policy, environmental policy. However, these risks occurrences are resulting in the relationship of cause and effect events. These events are not directly observable.

Such as, the complexity of relationship between terrorism and airline profitability. Hence, if global airline industry can predict when those risks occur to do protective strategic behavior. It is possible that which can understand why these risk events will occur and their protective strategic behaviors also influence their outcomes to be positive to avoid any external risk threats on the long term. However, I think hierarchy, self supply airline organization efficiency methods which are as possible predictors of user preferences to avoid risk threat events to cause whose airline businesses failure occurrences in airline industry because it can reduce oil shortage factor which causes their air ticket prices need to be rised to keep their planes can have enough fuel supply.

- Why tourism and airline industries have close relationship to influence their profitability between of them.

In my study, I suppose terrorism, profitability and the price of petroleum which had properties of distinct and interrelated close relationship. Moreover, these variables (terrorism, profitability and the price of petroleum) displayed differentiation, self replication, efficiency and hierarchy which can cause risk events to airline industry. However, I also think the other internal and external threat factors of airline industry, such as inflation, bank interest rate, business model, service quality, airline fuel or plane engine technology, air ticket pricing, brand loyalty, airline strategic management, government policy and fuel hedging of these factors which can also raise the risks to threaten any airlines existence in airline industry.

There are two basic business models in airline industry. They are network (full service) and low cost (discount) carriers. The network carrier model employs diversification strategy by increased domestic destinations, serving international routes, providing diverse seating arrangements (business, economy and first class), maintaining a complex system of offering high quality service. Otherwise, low cost (discount) airlines focus on lower air fares. To keep operating costs down, discount airlines offer shorter routes and provide point-to-point destinations rather than through sophisticated flights are primarily in domestic destinations. So, discount airlines operate a common model aircraft fleet, offer a single seating arrangement and cheaper flight services offered to compare network airlines. However, these two basic business models have their unique competitive abilities to provide any airlines existence in airline industry nowadays.

In fact, natural resource of oil is decreasing in our earth. But as the same time, human demand is increasing and oil supply is decreasing, so it also causes the oil fuel price is increasing to supply to airline industry. It influences not only to airline industry, it also impacts of higher oil fuel price to tourism, such as expansion of airports are made based on expected demand increase.

Tourism has been proven to many adverse events, including terrorism, flight disruptions. Beside, the bad natural climate change influences, such as the volcanic ash cloud event occurred in April 2010 year. So, airline industry need to concern climate change because it will cause high fuel prices indirectly. For example, the event occurred the extreme increase in operating costs for airlines in 2008 year, due to unprecedented prices for aviation fuel also meant, that despite the introduction of fuel charges, so this event causes the global airline industry recorded losses seriously. Even if alternative fuels become commercially available for airlines which are still likely to be more expensive than present aviation fuel. Thus, it seems that poor tourism will influence poor travel consumption and low airline tickets sale.

Higher airfares in the future are likely to lead to reduction in travel and cause tourists to shift from more distant to closer destination. When some of the economic responses to higher oil prices are obvious assessing the overall economic impacts on tourism is difficult. However, long term changes in global oil price rises will be similar to global changes in other commodity prices, exchange rates and income. It is therefore important to consider the impact of high oil prices on tourism from a general equilibrium perspective rather than relying only on bottom partial equilibrium. However, I believe tourism and airline industries have close relationship, such as tourism and airline industries are likely to suffer in an environment of high oil prices. Given that tourism destinations receive tourists from a range of origins, it would be useful to understand of some countries are increasing oil prices than others. Such as the net oil importing countries are selling higher oil prices than oil exporting countries generally. For example, New Zealand is an oil import country to provide planes for international visitor arrivals, so its oil fuel price is usually higher to charge to NZ airlines because any NZ airlines need to pay to foreign countries to buy any oil more expensive price. So, NZ airlines usually charge higher airfares to its visitors to compare the other exporting oil countries' airlines.

In economic theory, on income effects indicate negative impacts on tourism demand, the exact effects of higher oil fuel prices for specific destinations are far from clear. However, airline industry's different market segments show different sensitivities to air ticket fares changes. On the first hand, if the visitors are long destinations generally wealthier than average and therefore potentially less affected, as energy costs would be a smaller proportion of their income compared will be those from less wealthy groups. On the second hand, oil prices don't translate into higher transport costs especially not on air routes that are highly competitive and that are maintained for strategic reasons. On the third hand, many other factors shape tourists' decision making, including emotion drivers or those related to images, fashions and perceptions.

Increasing environmental protection awareness of tourists could also be an important factor to influence tourism consumption, instead of oil fuel price raising causes air ticket fares raising factor to reduce traveler numbers. However, oil price raising reason causes also due to high use of cars, vans and domestic air transport in some countries, e.g. Hong Kong, China countries, there are many people like to buy cars to drive. So, the private driver numbers are increasing demand to cause these countries' oil fuel prices raise in the short time suddenly. It will influence HK and China air tickets prices need to be risen , due to there are many cars, vans and domestic air transport tools need to use oil to supply energy to cause oil import numbers will increase to HK and China and HK and China airlines need to pay higher price to buy oil to use. In the result, HK and China airlines air ticket prices will also need to rise and it will influence HK and China travel consumption desire.

Q3 Why can oil fuel raising price strategy cause risk to airline ?

In long run, implications of changes to supply and demand side conditions of oil fuel energy may differ qualitatively. For example, due to investment responses of producers, consumers and governments in alternative energy sources and more energy efficient plants, vehicles are supplied in order to achieve oil fuel price can't be risen seriously.

However, I believe oil fuel rising charge will be an important factor to influence global airline ticket fares to be also increased. Firstly, on the bank interest changing factor, e.g. bank interest rate rising which only attract more bank saving. But it can not influence the bank savers who choose to reduce relax time to go to other countries travelling. Otherwise, when the bank savers can save more money to earn higher interest in banks, who will prefer to choose to use their saving to consume travelling. Due to who can earn higher interest rate after a period of saving time. So, I believe whose behavioral travelling consumption will be raised when the banks will raise interest rate, then the bank savers won't choose to save more money in banks. So it is possible that who will withdraw more money to consume to go to travelling from their bank saving. It seems bank interest rate changing won't influence bank savers' behavioral travelling consumption to be reduced. Secondly, on the exchange rate changing factor, although any country's exchange changing will cause other countries' money value to be fallen down or risen up. However, it won't influence any travelers' behavioral consumption to be reduced seriously. Although, it is possible that the traveler won't spend too much to go to shopping when who travel to the another country and arrive the country. But, it is not possible to influence the traveler decides to reduce consumption to buy any air ticket to go to travelling. Thirdly, any country inflation also can not reduce travelers' travelling consumption easily because inflation can influence consumers who choose to buy cheaper foods and clothing and reduce entertainments in their every day life. But, one country's inflation can not influence it's citizen do not spend much travelling expenditure because travelers only spend one time or two times of travelling every year usually. So, the travelling expenditure rate of any households is not too much to compare daily essential expenditure. So, it seems that bank interest rate and exchange rate changing and inflation factors won't influence any travelers' travelling consumption of decisions to be reduced easily. Otherwise, if the oil fuel price raises too much, then global airlines' cost will be raised. So, the airlines only choose to increase their air fare prices to aim to avoid loss possibly. It seems that oil fuel price has direct influence airline income.

● Methods to solve rising air fare prices demand.

I. Why will biofuels energy be demanded ?

I suggest these methods how to avoid the oil raising price factor to cause airline air fare prices to be risen to lead the risk of traveler numbers to be reduced.

The first method: Whether aviation fuel markets will have what benefits from biofuels supply to planes. I shall refer the scope includes trends in jet fuel price, airline response to fuel price, increases and volatility and environmental goals for aviation. The aviation fuel supply industry includes production, distribution and consumption of aviation fuel and it outlines players in the aviation fuel supply chain. For example, at each airport, fuel supply chain organization and fuel sourcing could differ with regard to the role of oil companies, airlines, airport owners and operators and airport service companies. However, major jet fuel purchasers are airlines, general aviation operators, corporate aviation and the military, with most of the jet fuel in global different countries demanders being used for domestic commercial and civilian flights carrying passengers, cargos or both. Commercial aviation fuel efficiency has improved dramatically over time, largely due to aircraft and engine upgrades and operational and air traffic control improvements. So, it seems that fuel supply factor can influence airline fare prices majorly.

However, jet fuel prices generally correlate with prices of crude oil and other refined petroleum products, such as diesel. So, increasing prices and the persistent price volatility of jet fuel markets import airline industry finances in any countries. However, airlines use various strategies to manage aviation fuel price certainty, including financial hedges, increased vertical integration and adjustments in aircraft utilization and size to avoid the jet fuel raising price risk. Investments in alternative aviation fuel could be a mechanism to diversity expose to the price of petroleum. It seems the use of alternative aviation fuel would serve to diversify the fuel mix to reduce the risk of jet fuel monopoly raising price threat. If a diversified fuel mix were to avoid either fuel raising price in short term or to avoid fuel raising price in long term. Potential benefits include reduced actual fuel costs from only choice of jet fuel supply increased price certainty and lessened fuel costs. This diversify could allow airlines to become more consistently profitable and to make other investments in their businesses.

So, biofuels have potential to meet aviation industry needs, possibly including managing risks of upward fuel price trends and fuel price volatility and avoid risks with greenhouse gas emissions. So, the aviation fuels market could use biofuels to reduce greenhouse gas emission and mitigate long-term upward price trends, fuel price volatility or both.

What are the challenges of high priced oil for aviation? In fact, nowadays not the resources of oil as such, but much more the insecurity of supply, due to geopolitical instability in combination with a tight oil market makes a scenario with much higher oil prices than the world is currently experiencing not unlikely. Aviation is completely dependent upon oil as its fuel source. Since no practical energy substitute is readily available for commercial aviation, a scarcity of petroleum relative to demand will present a major aviation policy. In addition, efficiency gains, due to operational measures and new aircraft medium term. In particular, it has been demonstrated that the annual reduction rate in fuel consumption traffic unit is not a constant, but is itself also falling, in contrast to past estimates.

So, a high-priced oil scenario will have severe consequences for demand, airline revenues, the competitive position of airports and eventually airline networks, strategies and fleet development. In particular, transfer demand, short-haul and leisure traffic can be expected to be heavily affected by high oil prices, due to their relative high price sensitivity. So, different countries' governments or/and airlines are valuable to research another new and potential biofuel energy to substitute oil energy to supply our planes to reduce the threat of oil monopoly supply to influence the cause of air fare raising prices. Because the elasticity is very high to travelers, when the travelers feel air fares are rising high or even low level to influence travelers who will choose not to buy the air tickets to go to travel easily.

Will the fuel (oil based inputs) risk be higher to compare other costs to cause air ticket prices to be increased?, e.g. engineering maintenance, employees salaries, general cleaning, security office expenses etc. expenditures to airlines? If the probability-weighted upside effect on firm value when a risk is resolved favorably is greater the risk than the probability-weighted downside effect if the risk is resolved badly, then expected value work not be enhanced by hedging. So, the risk will be resolved badly to any commercial airlines. Airlines are an interesting case because the direct effect of source of risk resides squarely within the no offset in revenue functions (unlike for oil producers, for example), so value effects from costs feed directly into equity value. Most directly, the risk source is fuel costs to commercial airlines. Jet fuel is of course, a mix product of crude oil, so airlines indirectly face oil price risk. There are reasons to expect that airlines' fuel costs might to convex in oil price (i.e. absent any hedging). For example, oil prices, being generally pro-cyclical in recent times, tend to be highest when airline demand is strong. Airlines are therefore apt to use more high priced fuel than low-priced fuel over time. Airlines can raise air fare benefit is limited by the elasticity of demand. Also, cost functions could be influenced from fuel cost corresponds to upturns in economic activity overall (due to demand pressures on oil related prices), so it causes that airline's capacity delivers their services given their level of fixed capital. The essence of airlines basis risk in the case of jet fuel is essentially the time profile of the refining margin between crude and jet fuel, or the time profile of the price differential between other refined distillates and jet fuel. Thus, it is far from clear that risk management with oil is sure to add value to any airlines. It seems the impact of airline energy and any countries' domestic or foreign airline passenger travel numbers which have direct close relationship.

Q4 What factors will influence airline industry's price elasticity of supply and demand?

In fact, the airline industry is largely dependent on the supply of the oil industry. Otherwise, the oil industry is inelastic. However, the increase or decrease of the price of airfare is directly related to the increase or decrease of the oil's price to fuel the aircrafts because there has no any new energy which can be substituted to oil fuel to airline industry. So, it seems oil fuel producers are monopolies to control its sale price to be raised easily.

Another factor that can affect airline industry to be directly targeted by a tragedy brought about by terrorism. The past four years, from 2001 year to 2005 year, there had been at least $40 billion worth of losses in the airline industry because of the September 11 date terrorism attacks in 2000 year. There had been an expected and significant decrease in the demand for the airline industry services because of the attacks that involved planes hijacking and crashing into key locations like the World Trade Center and the Pentagon in USA. Although, terrorism attacks can bring risk to influence fuel price rising in airline industry. However, this risk occurrence to airline industry is only that after the terrorism attacks occurred. It is possible that terrorism attacks won't occur again in the future.

Otherwise, our concerning ought be the greenhouse emissions and how it affects global warming. The air quality would be better once this new regulations are adopted. However, it would affect large airlines. So, it would increase the price of airfares because of economic fees that airline companies have to cover. Air pollution can give a negative impact on the domestic or oversea owned airline companies for long term. If airlines' planes can use clean fuel to fly, e.g. biofuel, then it will bring benefits to global airlines for long term. On the positive side, the environment would be healthier as the earth's temperature would rise, and greenhouse effect would be dramatically reduced. This positive effect can come at a cost that is greater than most people perceive. So, the environment protection travellers who will reduce travelling times to avoid air pollution is caused to influence human health. It seems that airlines need to concern to apply psychological method to predict whose travelling consumption of behavior which is more suitable than behavioral economy method.

On the psychology view point on travelers, who will be more preferable to catch planes to go to different countries to travel, due to the chance of air pollution and global environmental warm issues will be reduced to low risk to influence our health if planes can use biofuel to be energy to fly in the future one day. It seems that spending expenditure to research other non polluted biofuel new energy is one solvable method to global airline industry in the future. To solve, any airlines or countries' governments or oil producers ought choose to spend more time to research new biofuel. Otherwise, the predicting when terrorism attacks event will be occurred, it is more difficult to predict the time more than researching to produce new biofuel energy method in the future.

So, I recommend that researching the new biofuel energy or other kinds of energy to substitute the oil energy and air pollution risk these two factors are the urgent behavioral economy method is used to solve this challenge which the airlines or oil producers or different countries' governments which need to concern nowadays. Because these two negative environment factors are the most influential to cause traveller individual travelling consumption desire to be fallen among of other negative environment factors.

Q5 Can facility management strategy bring benefits to raise productive efficiency to organizationsFacility management benefit to office workplace ?

In private organizations, when the firm has facility management department, whether it can bring efficient administration to influence clerks to work efficiently in office, e.g. reducing administrative time or shorten time to work in administrative processes, in order to achieve minimizing clerk number labor cost. How to design office facilities to let office staffs to feel comfortable to work and reducing their pressure to work. It seems that office working environment will influence office staff individual performance. If the office working environment could improve efficiency and creativity of services to satisfy office workers' comfortable working environment needs. It will reduce every administration manager's working pressure when he/she needs often to find methods to attempt to encourage whose administrative clerks to avoid to waste working time to do some non-major administration tasks. Hence, how to design or allocate or arrange office any facilities' stored locations or whether how many equipment number is the enough to store in the locations, which will influence office employees' working attitude in order to raise or reduce their administration tasks efficiency indirectly, e.g. the office is clean or dirty, whether office reception has enough information telephone switchboard operation facilities, whether every clerk's table has enough computers number to supply to every to use, whether internet speed is fast or slow in order to let any employees can send and receive email to communicate or download any document from internet in short time, whether data processing and computer system maintenance service supply is enough to be repaired to employees' computers immediately when their computers are broken to wait repair, whether website editing facilities operation whether is enough to link to office every staffs in order to let any office staffs can apply internet to do their tasks conveniently in short time.

Hence, all of these general office equipment facilities whether they are enough supplied and their stored positions anywhere are the suitable to assist any clerks to work conveniently, they will influence every office employee's administrative and productive efficiency indirectly as well as all faxes, copying machines, computers, whether internet linking maintenance service time is short or long to prepare to any office employees to use conveniently any time, these different issues will also influence every employee individual efficiency in office. Hence, it concludes that office working environment, facilities supply number, facilities maintenance service and facilities location storing both factors will influence employee individual administrative productive efficiency in office.

- facility management benefits to service working environment

Can effective facility management improve service working environment to raise employee individual work performance? It is a concern about the quality of service to its customer question. The term" standards and goals" are often used to measure staff individual service performance whether he/she can serve to customers to let them to feel this staff's service performance or attitude is good or bad.

Is the service workplace working environment facilities enough, it will influence customer service staff individual performance.

For shopping center service industry case example, for this situtation, e.g. shopping center's facilities are enough or are placed to the suitable locations in order to let the shopping center's customers to feel comfortable to shopping when they enter this shopping center as well as whether the shopping center's facilities can influence the customer service staffs to serve whose shopping customers easily or difficult, due to whether the shopping center's facilities whether are adequate supplied or their locations are the best suitable positions to influence their service performance to let them to feel easier or comfortable to serve their customers in any large size shopping centers. For example, whether the lamps' lighting energy is enough to let the shoppers to feel safe to walk to visit any shops when there are many shoppers were walking to cause crowd and they feel difficult to walk to avoid any body contact to any one in busy time when the shopping center has no enough lights to let them to see anywhere in the shopping center's dark environment. Then it will influence customer service staffs to feel difficult to find any shopping center customers, e.g. when two shopping center customers are fighting in one location where is far away to the shopping customer service staffs and securities in the shopping center, because the shopping center is large and it has no enough light to let the customer service staffs and securities to find their frighting location to deal their fighting behavior and other shopping center's shoppers will feel very dangerous to walk their fighting location to avoid to close them. Then, it will has possible to cause death or hurt to any one of these two fighting shoppers ,even other shoppers' life. Because the shopping center's securities and customer service staffs who need to spend much time to find their fighting location, it will delay they can bring the policemen to their fighting location when they arrive this shopping center's destination in short time in order to solve their fighting behavior to influence all shoppers' life in this shopping center. Hence, the shopping center whether it has enough lamps number and the lamps' light whether is enough, these lighting facilities will influence any shopping center customer service staffs and securities who can spend less time to arrive any locations to deal any urgent matters.

For another situation in shopping center, if the shopping center has no enough paying telephone service facilities to supply shoppers to phone to anyone when they feel need to phone to any in the shopping center. Then, it will lead to some shoppers decide to find where the shopping center's reception's telephone to supply to them to phone call to anyone. If they are ten shoppers are waiting to use the shopping center's reception telephone to phone call to their friend or family within one minute. Thus, it will influence the reception customer service staffs feel difficult to arrange how to distribute the only one telephone to these ten shoppers to use to phone call their friend or family when they are queuing within their one minute waiting time in the shopping center's reception. If these ten shoppers can not use the reception telephone to phone call anyone. hen, they will feel dissatisfactory and complain to the reception service staffs politely. So, lacking enough facilities in the shopping center's any where, it will possible to influence their shopping centers' shoppers to feel all shopping center's service staff individual performance to be poor. It means that if the shopping center expects to improve customer satisfaction to its customer service staff's behavioral performance, it meets have enough facilities to be supplied in the shopping center to let its shoppers to feel it is one comfortable and safe shopping center. In conclusion, shopping center's facilities will have possible to influence shoppers' feeling to evaluate its customer service staffs to evaluate whether their service attitudes are good or poor indirectly.

- Can facility management improve productivity

The productivity means resources (input) is therefore the amount of products or services (output), which is produced by them. Hence, higher (improved) productivity means that more is produced with the same expectation of resource, i.e. at the same cost is terms of land materials, machine, time or labor. Alternatively, it means same amount is produced at less labor cost in term of land, material, machine, time for labor that is utilized. So, it brings this question: How can facility management improve productivity? I shall explain as these several aspects, it is possible to be improved productivity from (FM) successfully.

Improved productivity of farm land: If the farming land has better facility management to bring advantages by using better seed, better facilities of cultivation and most fertilizer. It is in the agricultural sense is increased (improved). So, facility management can bring benefits to any land resource to raise productivity in possible. It implies that the productivity of land used for better facility management of industrial purposes is said to have been increased if the output of products or service within that area of industrial land is increased output aim.

Improved productivity of material: If the factory has improved better equipment by facility management method to assist skillful workers to raise the manufacture cloth number, then the productivity of the cloth number is improved by (FM) method.

Improved productivity of labour: When the factory has good manufacturing equipment facilities to be supplied to improve methods of work to product more producing number per hour, then (FM) improved productivity of worker. Hence, in any workplaces, when organization has good facilities, it will influence employees to raise productivities in possible, because they need often to improved equipment facilities manufacture products to achieve higher production number aim.

- Can facility management raise bank employee productivity

Bank workplace environment is busy, the bank counter service staffs need to contact many bank clients to help them to serve or withdraw money from bank's counters. Whether does the quality of environment in bank workplace will influence the determination level of employee's motivation, subsequent performance productivity in bank working environment. For example, if the bank's staffs need work under inconvenient conditions , it will bring low performance and face occupational health diseases causing high absenteeism and turnover.

In general, bank size is usually small, it will have many bank clients enter bank to contact counter staffs to need them to help them to save or withdraw money. So, it will bring air pollution the crowd queue in every bank counter challenge when the bank has many people are queue waiting in counters to queue. So, bank working condition problem relates to environmental and physical factors which will influence every bank counter staff individual working performance to serve bank clients satisfactory. However, bank staffs need to deal many documents concern every client personal data every day. So, they need to spend much time to use computer and painting machines. This is particularly true for these employees who spend most of the day operating a computer terminal in bank workplace. As more and more computers are being installed in workplaces, an increasing number of business has been adopting designs for bank offices installment. So, bank needs have effective facilities management design because of demand of bank staffs for more human comfort.

An good equipment facility management for bank staffs to use conveniently, it is assumed that better workplace environment can motives bank employees and produces better productivity. Hence, bank office environment can be described in terms of physical and behavioral components to influence bank staffs to work inefficiently. To achieve high level of bank employee productivity, bank organizations must ensure that the physical environment in conductive to bank different department organizational needs, facilitating interaction and privacy, formality and informality, functional and disciplinarily, e.g. house loan or private loan departments, counter service department, visa card application department.

Thus, in a high safe privacy facility management working environment will let different department bank staffs feel safe to worry about privacy loss in possible. So, the improving bank facility to bring safe and high privacy to avoid bank client individual loss in working environment issue, the facility management can be results to bring these benefits, such as in a reduction in a number of complaints and absenteeism and an increase in productivity.

- Can (FM) create value to organization?

(FM) can reduce managing facilities as a strategic resource to add value to the organization and its overall performance, e.g. saving the energy in building and take care of shuttle buses and parking facilities space management for , on economic efficiency and effectiveness, or good price and value for the organization.

If the organization expects to apply (FM) process to save energy, it depends on possible input factors, i.e. interventions in the accommodation facilities services. So, it seems that the organization expects to save its energy consumption in its building. It needs have good space management facilities between parking its shuttle buses in its property's car park.

Why does space facility management is important to influence efficiency and productivity. For one school's building example, when the school decides none of the two gymnasiums student sport entertainment centers to be built in order to reduce financial cost and higher benefits. Remarkably, the use of space with the school overall strategic goals , such as creating spaces that better can support the teaching, motivate students and teachers, attract more students and increase the utilisation of existing space to accommodate an increasing number of students.

If it hopes to make high quality teaching facilities on student's choice where to study. The school will need to choose to build either one comfortable and new design facility teaching accommodation or build two gymnasium sport entertainment centers in its limited land space either for students' learning or sport aim. Due to it feels new teaching accommodation can make more attractive to increase students numbers to choose it to study more than building two new gym sport centers to let them do sport in school.

Hence, space choice (FC) management strategy will be one important considerable issue, when the organization has limited land space resources to make choose to build any constructions in order to increase many clients number. Such as the school organization has limited storage land resource to let it to build either two gymnasium sport entertainment centers or one new teaching accommodation in order to attract many students to choose it to learn. Hence, it needs to gather data to make more accurate evaluation to decide how to apply its space facility to choose to build these both kinds of buildings in order to achieve the attractive student learning choice aim, so whether the two sport entertainment activity centers or one new teaching accommodation choice, it needs to gather information to decide whether the school ought to choose to build which kind of building in order to achieve the increase of student number aim, so space facility management will be this school's land shortage problem.

Q6 How can Property facility management strategy influence householder buying behavior ?

One new property's low price is attractive factor to influence property buyer individual preference choice. Does the new individual's facility management factor influence the property buyer's preference choice decision, if the property buyer feels its facility management is better than other similar properties, even it's price is higher than other properties. I shall indicate some cases to analyze this possibility as below:

Some properties' facility management service quality has possible to create true value for any property buyers when they consider the calculation ingredients to make decision whether to new property has higher value to choose to buy. The factors may include: price, natural environment, transportation tools convenient available, shopping centers supplies, the neighour quality, and the property's internal facility management etc. factors.

In fact, car or house purchase buyers, they have similar behaviors. It is that car's buyers will consider the car's machines whether they are safe to drive on roads, instead price, manufacture loyalty factors. It is possible that the car's machines quality factor will be preference to any car buyers when they make preference decisions to choose which brand its cars are the suitable. However, if the car's brand is famous and its appearance beautiful and price is cheap. But the car consumer feels its machine qualities are unsafe to let the driver to drive on road. Then, the car's poor machine quality factor will influence the car buyer's decisions to choose to buy this car. It can influence the car buyer individual car purchase decision.

The car buyer's behavior is similar to property buyer's behavior. Although, the new property price is cheap, good neigh ours are living near to the new property's location, shopping centers and transportation tools are available to near to this new property's area. But if the property buyers' feels its facility management is poor quality to compare other similar properties. Then, the poor quality of facility management factor will have possible to influence the property buyers whose final buying decision to choose to buy this new property. It brings this question: How and why can the facility management poor quality factor influence property consumers' preference choice?

In general, all property consumers won't know whether the new property's facility management is good or bad quality , they need to spend time to visit to the new property in order to observe whether its internal facility is satisfactory to his/her acceptable level. In simple, their purchase decision will regard to how to allocate household budget, how the household's economic resources are influenced, e.g. for travelling, visits to restaurants, comparing the different similar types of property product groups, e.g. apartments or houses or houses of a givn size data. For example, if one property's room(s) size is (re) small to compare other kind similar product type of room(s) size. Although the prior property's price is cheaper to compare to the later properties. But, if some property buyers hoped the property has large room(s) size, then the later larger room(s) size which will be possible to some property buyer's preference choice. Even, their property price is more expensive to compare the smaller room(s) size of properties. Thus, the property's room size which will be one major factor to influence property buyers' purchase decision. room's size had relationship to facility management issue. Moreover, if the room's quality and design is attractive, then it will bring more attractive to persuade some property buyers to choose to buy them to live in preference.

Hence, whether the new property is good durable product feeling which will influence householder's choice. If the householder feels the new property has long term durable life to avoid to spend much maintenance expense when they have been living in the new property for a long term period. They will believe it has better facility management, quality to let them to live longer time and the most importance is that they do not need to spend any maintenance expense , due to the property 's any internal facilities are damaged easily.

The external factors may include: culture, reference groups, family, social class and demography of lifestyle as well as internal factors may include: feelings, past property buying and living experience , property knowledge, motivation of the property buyer individual psychology. These both factors can influence any property buyer individual decision making process to do final house purchase behavior. However, internal factors, such as: property knowledge of facility management and property living experience, e.g. how to evaluate to choose to buy the property , due to the property buyer's past living experience for the past property's facilities whether its facilities can satisfy its property buyers' comfortable living needs. This internal factor will be more important to influence any property buyer's property purchase final decision. If he/she feels whose prior old property's facilities are satisfactory. Then, he/she will compare this new property and old property's facilities to decide whether this new property is value to buy. So, the old property's facility will be the measurement standard to compare his/her next new property purchase choice. So, the property purchaser will compare these new and old property's property facilities product knowledge to similarities among property alternative which will influence his/her final decision to choose to buy the new property to live.

It seems that property low price factor must not guarantee to attractive many property buyers' choice. Otherwise, it is assumed that many property buyers like rent or buy to live the property for themselves for long term intention. There are less property buyers expect to sell the first property to earn profit intention. So, they will usually consider whether the property is long term durable product to avoid to pay maintenance expense when they had been living in the property in long term.

Some factors that taking consideration are proximity to the specific location, housing prices, developer's brand, the payment scheme, reference group, which are not the main factors to influence any property buyer individual choice. Because property buyer's need is that the property has good facilities to supply to them to live, e.g. good heater equipment can provide hot water to them to bath in winter or good air conditioners can provide cold temperature to let them to feel cool comfortable feeling in summer in their homes. Good electric tools facilities , when they have need to use electricity in safe environment at home, e.g. car park accessibility facility , level of security facility , surface area facility and housing types, bedroom, bathroom facilities, quality of housing manufacturing raw material, house design , house durable guarantee, speed of complaint responsiveness, specification accuracy, confirmation of building plan service, showing legal file property purchase process service, finance instalments process assistance, speed of responsiveness, officers' skills of presentation. All of above these concern property facility management issues will influence any property buyers' final choice to decide whether the property is value to buy. So, facility management will influence property purchaser individual final decision in possible.

Q7 Can facility management strategy can raise workplace productivity ?

Facility management is one part of manufacturers or retailers as their productivity in workplace as their input and functionalistics within physical environment. In fact, facility management in workplace may include: site selection, property disposal, site acquisition, workplace space allocation, space inventory, space forecasting facility management, interior furniture change planning, interior furniture installation, moving maintenance, inventory, design evaluation, employment satisfaction evaluation plan, external maintenance and breakdown maintenance, preventive maintenance, landscape maintenance, energy space facility management, hazardous waste disposal, capital , operating furniture budgeting. So, it seems that one workplace considered whether the workplace's facility is enough to let employees to work in order to raise efficiency and improve productive performance more easily. Then, it will bring this question:

- How and why workplace facility management can influence consumer individual satisfaction?

Strategic FM delivery is essential for business survival. I shall explain why for delivery is important to influence customer satisfaction. In business process view point, an effective and meaningful service to their customer , i.e. the user. For logistic industry, the product's delivery time will influence when the product can be sent to the user's arrival destination. If the product is delayed to sent to the user's home or office or any location destination. The reason is because the logistic product sender has no efficient facility management (FM) arrangement in its warehouse . Then, its warehouse lacks efficient (FM), which will cause users to feel its delivery service is poor and they will complain its delivery service staffs. Then, they will find another delivery service company to replace its service. So, it explains that logistic industry's warehouse (FM) service arrangement can raise efficient time to send any products to their customers in order to let they feel satisfactory service. For example, Amazon online logistic company's warehouse has applied artificial intelligence robotic tools to assist warehouse workers to arrange the different kinds of products to deliver to the right shelves . Then, the warehouse robotics will follow their right product shelves locations to follow the right products to deliver to US domestic or overseas product buyers in the short time and it can avoid the wrong products to deliver to the wrong buyers' risk. Also, the (AI) delivery tools can raise time efficiency to assist Amazon warehouse workers to reduce their work load, and tried to work in large warehouse environment. Although, its warehouse's area is large, the (AI) tools facility can help them to deliver the different products to different shelves in the right locations , e.g. exact product number and the kinds of product to be delivered to the right country' client's shelf location in the warehouse. Also, it implies FM is very important to influence Amazon warehouse delivery efficiency and avoiding delivery wrong occurrence chance. For example, the shelf location belongs to US domestic customers, or the shelf location belongs to Japan customers, or the shelf location belongs to Hong Kong customers, or any other Asia or Western countries' different customers' locations. The warehouse's facility needs have different countries' shelves enough space to put and it also need enough space to let the (AI) tools, robotic delivery workers and human workers both to walk to different shelves locations easily and the different countries' shelves number needs to be calculated accurate. For example, it has how many client number will buy Amazon's the kind product per day. If it has above 5,000 to 10,000 China clients to buy the kind of product. Then, it will need to make judgement how many shelves are placed in the warehouse. So, it can avoid to lack enough shelves to put any different kinds of products to prepare to delivery to China clients in efficient time and it won't avoid to delay to deliver to their homes or offices or any locations in China.

Hence, such as Amazon logistic case, it explains why warehouse's space shelves number and area or locations facility management can influence workers or (AI) delivery tools how to move convenient and avoiding the delivery to the customer's wrong destination chance occurrence and shortening time to deliver products to its clients efficiently. Then, due to the delivering time is shorten and the wrong delivery destination's occurrence chance is also reduced , even it can avoid to deliver the product to wrong client's destination occurrence. Then, the logistic firm's clients will feel more satisfactory to its product sale delivery service and their complaints will be avoided. Hence, it explains effective warehouse (FM) space management service arrangement is essential to any logistic businesses nowadays.

- Facility management brings departmental benefits

Why do organizations need have facility management (FM) service? As above examples indicate that (FM) can improve workplace environment facilities, e.g. warehouse environment to let workers to raise efficiencies or improve performances, even it can influence consumers to raise satisfactory to it's services indirectly, also it can help organizations' equipment to be used long term to cause old and are needed to spend expenditure to maintenance or change new equipment in order to improve better quality . So , it can assist organizations to avoid to spend more expenditure for new equipment purchase or maintenance. All these issues will be facility management service's benefits to an organizations, which can concern raising customers' service satisfaction, raising efficiency or improving productive performance, raising productivity, reducing equipment or property maintenance or new alternation much of expenditure spending, office or warehouse or any workplace space planning arrangement .

However, every organization will need a facility manager or manage whose team effectively . When a facility manager begins to apply FM techniques to solve business problems. The case for FM is made. It is a simple matter of demonstrating a qualified return on the investment required. Every organization's success, FM operation of three key activities: they include: needing a proper understanding of the organization's needs, wants, drivers and goals and knowing when needs to review its changing circumstances, developing an effective facilities solution o support the organization's needs, wants , property drives and contribute to achieve its goals both short term and long term, achievement of reliable delivery of that solution in a managed, measured manner.

So, it bring one question: What are the influential factors to be followed the right direction to FM manager's strategic FM operational decision? The influencing factors may include: ownership, governance sector, complexity and perhaps of most significant, the size of the organization's property portfolio.

In fact, major occupiers feel FM service need, they are large corporate organizations and public service organizations. Their aims usually are to raise. The most marginal improvement in efficiency or effectiveness, these aims are the great significance. Major property occupiers will already have a facilities department or individuals performing the FM function with another department like property, finance or human resource, sale and marketing's facilities.

Usually these FM need occupiers who will encounter this problem: How can apply FM service systems and processes to be developed to improve reliable service delivery making use of the economies of scale, not suffering because of the size of the problem. This question will be facility manager individual concerning question: How to apply (FM) technique to solve the improvement reliable service delivery making use of the economics of scale problem for whose organization?

In reality much of external facilities management benefits to organizations, instead of raising efficiency, improving performance, raising productivity, reducing maintenance expenditure, e.g. energy saving, reducing natural resource waste, increasing local employment, improving supply chain management are all elements of the FM contribution to every organization's need. Hence are the work life balance argument and provision of an effective and safe working environment that supports why some organizations feel need (FM) service to support their organizational development.

Moreover, on cost benefit of space saving efficient view point, space service cost reduction is a key driver for all organizations and the medium, or large sized players will benefit directly from a well coordinated facilities strategy. For example, application FM technique to help warehouse or office space area to save 50% space vacancy to let employees can move easily or putting enough furniture or equipment or many stocks can be putted in warehouses . So, paying more rent expenditure to rent or purchasing another new warehouse or office to satisfy workers or employees' working environment to be better need. If the organization has effective (FM) technique, then it has enough space vacancy to supply to the increase stocks number to be putted inside in warehouse and it can let workers to move safety in available to let staffs to move easily and equipment have enough space to be stored in the limited warehouse space problem.

For greater space savings benefits will bring either long term renting or buying of increasing offices or warehouse number expenditure problem to any organizations, when the organizations' cost or renting or buying accommodation probably accounting for 60 to 70% of total occupancy cost . So a strategic program to release space or the prevent the acquisition of moves can be the most significant consideration to any facility manager, with between

40% and 60% of the workplaces are unoccupied in most offices or warehouses at any given moment in time.
Hence, how to apply (FM) technique to save space occupied areas for employment moving or stocks or equipment saving need in offices or warehouses. This issue will be any facility managers' seeking methods to solve problem. However, the important major advantage of facility management to organizations is that the application of management principle to keep the organization's property assets with the aim of maximizing their potentials. Thus, any organizations‘ facilities have become important, due to the property facilities' worth will increase if the organization's facility management technique can protect the organization's facilities have good performance. Then, the organization's maintenance expenditure will reduce and it won't need to spend expenditure to buy any new facilities to replace old facilities , due to they often damage factor when they are used old.

In conclusion, it explains why effective FM combines resources and activities can raise work environment improvement, which is essential to the raising employee performance aim. For hotel living service case example, this industry must need have good facility management service because hotels must need to fully equipped in term and facilities for effectiveness to satisfy hotel living clients‘ demand , hotels ought need good facilities asset management style lead to effectiveness in service delivery, there are benefit derivable from the adoption of facilities management from which other hotels can learn from for their effective operations. Hence, it explains why effective FM can bring benefits to hotels' properties to be more comfortable, beautiful appearances to attract many hotel customers to choose to live the hotel. Because hotel's building industrial kitchens, rooms facilities, equipment , halls of categories, restaurant facilities, gum sport entertainment centers‘ facilities, fans, elevators, lifts, electrical installation, escalators, baking equipment, recreational facilities, including golf courses which will be important factors to influence hotel clients' comfortable living feeling, if the hotel can keep its all facilities in the best living environment often. Then, it can raise chance to attract many hotel customers to choose it to live. So , hotel industry has absolute need to implement effective FM strategy to keep its properties more attractive to satisfy its clients‘ living needs.

Instead of hotel industry, logistic transportation industry also needs effective facilities management in warehouse, because of the logistic company's warehouse 's facilities are good, then it will assist to raise employee individual efficiency in the safe and system shelve stored facilities in workplace environment and improving performance.

Consequently, it will bring the shorten time to deliver any products to clients to avoide the delaying time delivery in order to let customers to feel more satisfactory to their services. In simple, it seems that some industries need have effective facilities management techniques to help them to bring long term customer satisfactory feeling, worker individual efficiency raising and performance improvement benefits. Hence, it seems facility management techniques' demand will be increased to some industries in popular in the future because it has help to raise employee individual efficiency , productive performance and client individual satisfactory level consequently.

CHAPTER TWO

Consumer psychology

Q1 How to attract travellers choose hotel room living service ?

What are some noticeable hotel service trends in the industry ? Travellers of today are diverse and want to stay in a place which lets them live out their individuality. They want a hotel which adapts to them, not the other way around. The quest for individualised experiences sets them apart from older generations and has created a challenge for many hoteliers. Guests expect convenience, simplicity and the same instant gratification they enjoy in other areas of their lives. However, hotel and resort staff face the daunting task of handling an endless array of guest issues with a limited team. No matter how well trained front desk staff might be, there are always occasions where long lines form and waiting guests become frustrated. Even a five-minute wait in a check-in line can result in a 50% reduction in guest satisfaction scores. Moreover, guests have become accustomed to the Airbnbs of the world where everything offered to them is extremely relevant and guest has the option to tweak the experience themselves. A similar trend is seen among major hotel chains, where they are using loyalty solutions to promote offers and services based on the guests' preferences and guests have the ability to check-in using mobile. Independent hotels are slowly but steadily starting to embrace such solutions. Personalisation of guest service is no longer a trend, but an obligation for hotels. For example, traditional check-in times were designed for a guest that no longer exists. With long haul travel now very much mainstream, 40% of guests are either arriving on flights before 7AM or leaving on flights that take off after 6PM. Tailoring check-in/check out times to your guest's travel plans is the next battleground of personalisation."

What's the power of automation for hotels and guests?

By combining powerful segmentation with a high-conversion platform, upselling can really help deliver the five R's of revenue management: Selling the right room on the right channel to the right customer at the right time at the right price. Using segmentation properly allows you to target and market to a variety of potential buyers with varying needs, behaviors and budgets. Doing this well will provide you data needed to understand the success of your current revenue strategies and adjust them to maximise your topline in the future. Software providers can take most of that work off your hands. Setting up your segments is done in a matter of minutes, and the software handles the rest, like making sure the segments you choose are offered attractive deals in automatically sent emails."

Can AI platforms or chatbots raise travellers living hotel room choice need ?
Artificial Intelligence (AI) platforms or chatbots can be used to answer simple guest questions and requests freeing up hotel staff to focus on the most complicated guest issues. With mobile keys, bluetooth technology allows mobile devices to communicate directly with the door lock on a guest room.Automation technology can also be leveraged to enhance communication between the hotel staff and guest. Platforms like ours at OpenKey also gives hotels the ability to offer mobile dining, valet requests, concierge, and other guest services – in addition to a digital key – from a mobile app.

I believe that AI technology can boost your hotel brand perception. Automating guest communication opens up a tremendous potential for the hotel. Typically pre-arrival or confirmation emails have been seen as just a system-generated message verifying that a reservation has been made. But this is the first time guest hears about you. "Wouldn't it be nice, if you could delight the guest with a warm greeting, in their own language, with offers that are specific to their profile or segment? With proper tools, this can be easily achieved. For exmaple, if a guest booked a standard room, the system may automatically offer the deluxe room. Or if the airport is far away, offer them a fully arranged taxi service. If targeted properly, upsell and cross-sell efforts can significantly improve guest satisfaction as offers are more relevant. When should you send the offer and who should you send it to? Hotels often send their upsell offers too early when the pain point the hotel is looking to solve is not front of mind for the guest. How should you change your offer depending on the nature of the guest? We'll change how we target and what we offer guests depending on nationality and travel time.

Moreover, AI technology is helping hotels to be more efficient. From the perspective of some hotels which apply AI technology, these hotels look to elevate their service, mobile technology will help us deliver a simplified and efficient guest experience. Today's traveller wants to save time and enjoy their travel, not wait in check-in lines. These hotels could help their customers can be happier about adding a tech solution that will ultimately benefit to their per booking hotel rooms service before they catch pair planes to arrive their country. So, they do not need to spend much time to find the best suitable hotel to live when the hotel can apply AI technology to help them to make hotel choice decision. For example, hoteliers are slowly beginning to understand that technology is not here to replace the human touch but to complement it. Historically guest-facing technology was seen as a toy they can live without. But more and more guests expect these types of convenience services and hotels are realising, this is the new norm. Most guests are not overly expressive about their wants and needs. This means, without tech, it will become extremely difficult to deliver superior guest experience.

How important is connectivity for hoteliers and the platforms they use? As a minimum we need the reservation data from hotel guests, which can be gleaned from the PMS, channel manager, or OTA. So it's important these systems are able to integrate easily with each other. Connectivity is the most important influential factor: Without it any lacking AI technological communication assistance hotels can't automate their services for their clients, which means adding manual work to the hotel's front desk, which simply doesn't work. The ability for technology to continue to help hotels run their businesses, hinges on the providers ability to connect into the hotel's tech stack. Moreover, hoteliers completely understand the pivotal role of tech, but their hands have been tied by the lack of connectivity offered by their incumbent technology systems.

On conclusion, hotel management is about overseeing every operation of the property. This requires knowledge of distribution strategy, finance, customer service, staff management, marketing, and more. Effective inventory management for hotels involves both creating and managing demand, and maximising returns. Revenue management is another huge part of managing your hotel. How do you get more money coming in and achieve business goals?

In the hospitality industry almost everything revolves around the customer, and they're the quickest party to point out any flaws. Good management eliminates as many mistakes as possible. Hotel management sometimes also requires the management of a restaurant. Turn your hotel restaurant into a premium dining experience that focuses on the whole package including the food, lighting, music, decor, and wine lists. This way, your restaurant won't only be the bait to bring new customers in, but also an incentive for current guests to return when they revisit the area.

Similar to search engines such as Google, OTAs have their own algorithms for how your property will rank, meaning you need to pay close attention to how you build your profile on them. Fighting food waste at your hotel goes beyond feeding people and helping the environment – it also improves your property's bottom line. Reporting on performance is essential to hotel management. You need to collect and analyse accurate data regularly to see where things are working, and what you need to improve on. Hotel management software is technology that allows hotel operators and owners to streamline their administrative tasks while also increasing their bookings in both the short- and long-term. Managing a hotel isn't all about managing the physical property, it's also about managing intangible things like reputation. There are many apps in the market to help with everyday challenges. Organised teams get more done and having everything under control also gives you a better grip on the overall success of the business.

● How and why hotel managers need to attempt to predict customer booking hotel room behavior or booking hotel room need psychology?

Any hotel management ought need to learn how to predict hotel entertainment consumer individual need in order to attract consumer living choice or increase consumers number easily. I assume that if the hotel can provide the room living service can let any hotel consumers to feel such ad themselves homes feeling. It will influence them to live longer time to stay in the hotel (prolonging hotel room booking days) in the hotel because they can feel themselves homes living feeling. How can make hotel room booking consumers to feel the hotel rocms are such as their homes living feeling? it is one interesting question to discuss. I shall explain as below;

Building hotel living holiday leisure feeling, this factor is very important to influence hotel living consumers to make final extending proplonging living consumers to make final extending or prolonging living days in the hotel. Holidays, by definition , are non-working times, an extended period of anticipated recreation, especially away from home, they can be days of festivity when no work is done. The prolem and opportunity for hotel living entertainment service providers, is that when hotel living customers are on holiday, or at leisure. Hotels need to give a chance of getting away from living holidays, new changing the batteries and for some a change of holiday living of entertainment lifestyle. Hence, if the hotel can let all customers to feel home comfortable living feeling to enjoy their one part of entertainment activity in the whole journeys. The hotel may persuade any one customer (hotel room living customers to prolong any one customer (hotel room living customers to prolong living days in the hotel).

Will the broad framework of leisure defined as time, there are many variations. In general, defining leisure as the time when someone is not working primarrily for money. So, if the hotel room living customer can feel that he/she spends the booking room living fee is value to choose the hotel room to live. The hotel room is such as unoccupied time or free time in whose journey time. Due to he/she feels that this living hotel room time is whose entertainment time. It is essential, then this unoccupied time may persuade him/her to prolong booking hotel room living time in the hotel. For example, he planned to stay 5 days in the hotel, but because he/she feels that the hotel can provide entertainment activities time to attract him/her to stay longer time in the hotel, e.g. gym sport facilities are very attractive sport playing entertainment or hotel restaurant can provide good taste food eating time in special dinner, breakfast, lunch time or swimming pool is beautiful design and large size and it can let him/her to feel actual natural beach environment feeling. Then, any one these extra entertainment facilities or services factors may influence any one customer to spend extending living time in the hotel. Such as this cause, this hotel living customer may feel need to live more two to three days, even more days in this hotel. Hence, hotel leisure as time psychological factor is also important to influence any one hotel room living customer to influence any one hotel oom living consumer to make extending living time decision easily, when they feel this hotel has themselves homes feeling.

Kraus & Bates (1975) add experiencing to the activity. Recreation consists of activities or experiences with are carried on volutarily in leisure time. They are chosen by participants, either for pleasure or to satisfy certain personal needs when provided as part of organized community programs, creation must be designed to achieve constructive goals.

Hence, if the hotel can consist any recreation actvities or experiences to let any one hotel living customer to enjoy to live when are carried on voluntarily in their leisure time. They can choose any kinds of leisure activities to play and live in the hotel, if the hotel any one kind of leisure activity can satisfy their leisure needs. Then, the hotel's any kind of leisure activity can achieve constructive goals to persuade any one hotel room living consumer likes to spend extra money to enjoy any kinds of hotel leisure facilties, instead of spending extra hotel room living expenditure to proplong hotel time in the hotel. Hence, it seems that whether the hotel can provide attractive leisure facilities to let consumers to relationship to influence they their long living or staying time in the hotel.

When asked what were the three most important factors in the development of hotel. Thus equality applied to most leisure facilities ideally, a public transport location may influence any one hotel room customer to choose which hotel location is the nearest to public transport in order to pay cheap transport fee to catch the public transport. This is one low transport fee cost factor to influence the potential hotel room customer choice.

Hence, any hotel's location will be chosen to build to near many public transport tools, e.g. buses, underground trains, taxis, trains station locations. It aims to attract the hotel room booking potential customers can pay cheap public transport fee to arrive their hotel conveniently. They do not need to spend long walking time to arrive their hotels after they catch any one kind of public transport tool to arrive their hotel destinations. Moreover, they do not need to spend long time to find where the hotel locates when they leave the bus stop. So, geographical location factor will be another main factor to influence hotel consumer choices.

The model is based on comparing demand and supply economc theory:

1. identifying where hotel demand is located, whether and to what extent, hotel rooms number demand exceeds hotel rooms number supply in the geographical area and whether , and where, the city has much land to provide space capacity to permit to build hotels number exists in the geographical area in the city.

2. Moreover, local demand is measured on the basis of the number of hotel visits per week in peack period for any hotel room needs determined by:

The total number of travelling visitors in the month rate , the demand rate, the proportion of residents who want to book room to live in the hotel, instead of overseas travelling visitors, the desired frequency of visits, how often overseas travellers want to visit the country and the proportation of visits which arise in the normal peiods per month, such as christmas, New Year etc. public holidays.

So, all of these hotel visitors public transport fee cheap demand number and hotel geographical locations, hotel entertainment facilities , hotel comfortable living feeling, hotel safety, hotel food taste, public holiday and visitor individual travelling need, air ticket price main factors which will influence any one hotel's room demand and supply number absolutely in behavioral economic theory view, instead of hotel environment and service performance basic element factor.

On conclusion, all of these any one element may influence any one hotel customers numner increases or decreases absolutely. Hence, any one hotel management can not neglect to learn how to implement their hotel management strategies effectively.

ref.

Kraus , R. & Batees , B. (1975). Creation leadership and supervision, W.B. Saunders, philadelphia, P.A.

How to supervise teams in hospitality industry

Any hotels need effective supervisors to supervise their teams in different department in order to raise service efficiency. How to supervise teams which is one important question to any hotels? I shall attempt to explain as below:

In hospitaloty industry, alomst everything depends on the psycical labour of many hours (non-managerial workers), waiters, mix drinks, wash dishes, checkquests, clean room, carry bags, mop floors, even security etc. All of these teams must need a supervisor to manage their make products and/or perform services. The human resources for personnel, and training departments are example of staffs who advise line departments, such as the food and beverage department on matters including hiring, disciplining and training.

In general, supervisor responsibility may include: achieving or exceeding the expected results, on time and on budget, planning or determining priorities. Organizing (scheduling), motivating (creative a positive work environment), controlling (monitoring and taking corrective action if mistakes are outside acceptable limits), communicating effectively.

In the reality, in a hotel you may have 5,000 minimum customers are day. You deal with your supervisors. You deal with your subordinates, and you deal with your guests, all coming at you from different directons. Salepeople , deliveries, inspectors, customer complaints and applicants . You jobs interrupt you. So , you are likely to have only a few seconds available when you make many important decisons.

You will feel bus to deal any of either above, these matters every day. Hence, in effective hotel organization, it needs have effective scientific management, it incudes these elements: Standardization, of work procedures, tool and conditions of work through design of work methods by specialists, careful selection of competent people, after training, and elimination of these (traineers) who could not or would not perform, complete and constant overseeing of the work, with total obedience from the worker‘ incenive pay for meeting the fair day for meeting the fair day’s work standard, the worker’s share of the increased productivity.

How to innovate hotel tasks to be work simplification or searching for the best way of performance tasks ? Supervisors can use time-and-motion study techniques, developing ways of simplifying tasks than often doubled or triples what a worker would do. This methods and principles had a great impact in food service kitchen, where work simplification techniques have been explored widely adopted. This methods ewere adopted although the idea that have hotel worker should share in the benefits of increased productivity seldom went along with the rest of the system. For example, in hotel kitcehen department , every cooking steep is systematized, and the cooker, dish cleaner is simply taught to run the kitchen dish cleaning machines, cooking machines follow the rules, and speak given phrases. When the kitchen bell rings, the cooker turns the hamburgers on dispenser one time, where is no room for deviation.

How a supervisor can build a positive work climate in his/her hotel department ? He/She needs to know his/her employee expectation and need. You may wonder whethet their performance will meet your expectation, and you may have some plans for improving productivity. But you may not realize that what there people expect from you and how you meet their expectations may have as much to do with their performance as your expectation of them. However, your staffs also expect you to be qualified to supervise. First, they want you to have worked in the area in which you are supervising: a hotel, room, a hotel kitchen, a hotel restaurant, lowing into a big motel from a job in a budget motel, you may also improve yourself. Your staffs want to feel that you understand the operation well and appreciate the work , they are doing. They want to feel that they and their jobs are in good hands, that you are truly capable of directing their work.

● Behavior modification supervising strategy

Behavior modification explains a newer method for improving performance. It explains all behavior is a function of its consequences; people behave as they do because of positive or negative consequences to them. If the consequences are positive, they will trend to repeat the behaviors, if they are negative, they will trend not to . Hence, if you are hotel kitchen cookers their supervisor, you need to give praise , or appreciation to the cookers , whose cooking skills can be improved when they can cook good taste foods ro satisfy hotel restaurant customer individual eatting feeling. Every time, you need to give praise to the excellent cooker’s cooking performance. Then, his/her cooking skills will be improved , due to your praise.

It is possible that he/she feels salary will be increased by your praise. Otherwise, when you feel the cooker's cooking skill is worse and your cookers their cooking foods taste are also worse and they can not satisy your cookers their customers' eatting taste needs often. Then , you ought not punish or blam to let him/her by your oral blaming or pubishment threat (without salary increasing threat). Consequently, his /her cooking skill can not be improved, even worse. You ought attempt to help him/her to find whether which aspects of cooking skills , he/she is felt to need to learn how to improve hir/her cooking skill to be better, and you ought teach him/her how to cool the kinds of food to be better taste. Consequently, his/her cooking skill will be improved by your teaching and patience excuse attitude.

● How to design clear job analysis?

Any one hotel team ought need have clear job analysis to let their departments supervisors and staffs to know whether what aspects of tasks , they need to do in order to achieve actual work performance improvement. For example, sever job units example, it may include: Stock service station, set tables, great quests, explain menu to customers, take food and beverage orders and complete guest check, pick up order and complete plate preparation, serve food, recommand wines and serve them, total and present check, perform side work, operate equipment , meet dress and grooming stantards, observe sanitation procedures and requirements, maintain good customer relations, and desired check arrange.

Hence, any one hotel restaurant server can know whether how they require the setting standards, training and evaluation jst as the actual work sequences do. Such units appears in ither jobs as well , and the same standards will apply in each case in the hotel any departments performance standards from the heart of the job description and they describe the what, how to and how wells of a job.

1. What the employee is to do?
2. How it is to be done?
3. To what extent it is to be done?

It means that any hotel department staffs and supervisors they need to know concern their job requirement such as : How much, how well, how soon. For example, " one waitor or waitress job at acertain restaurant. The server will take food and beverage orders for up to five tables with 100 % accuracy, using standard house procedures." It is the hotel restaurant waitor/waitress general job standard acceptance level.

Hence, waitor/waitress supervisor can folle this guideline to know how to supervise his/her staffs and evaluate whose job performance in the hotel restaurant.

On conclusion, due to hotel is one service industry, any hotel's different department effective supervising management, they need have good job standard, training and fair evaluation performance system, fair compensation and pubishment system, instead of the department supervisor whose supervising effort or ability whether is proficient or worse in order to influence whose team serving performance effectively and efficiently . However, any organization itself management team and supervising team will need have good communicating technique in order to let any department supervisor knows how to supervise his/her team effectively in order to achieve improvement service performance aim.

Q2 What are the differences between face reading technology and video camera recording consumer behavior predictive methods ?

The impact of emotions on judges, evaluations and decisions have long been important to psychology and consumer behavior on consumption. I shall examine how distinct perspectives shape the processes of appraisal that lead to emotional experience and how different consumers might define happiness distinctly. I examine emotions that vary by positive, negative and mixed. I also suggest new ways to distinguish among emotions and to assess how new ways to consumers to aim to be discovered by better understanding how consumers manage their experience of emotion to achieve their own affective goals. In my report, I shall indicate three aspects to research. The first aspect, I indicate how one sample technology to detect consumer emotion to predict facial reaction, such as Noldus Face Reader technology is used orange juice, sweets and chocolates confectionery foods or drinks to detect young consumers‘ emotion whether who like or dislike to eat or drink different brands of confectionery products from whose facial reaction for factory or shop experiments. Besides, how to use video cameras to record consumer individual behavior at home to predict why who choose to buy your product to help manufacturer, as you to predict why your clients choose to buy your products or choose not to buy products to use.

- Main Problem Being Addressed of face reading and video camera technology limits

Technologies that detect consumers' emotions can help companies to reduce the amount of money waste on unsuccessful product launches by stopping products before they are launched. Methods can be accurately measured consumers' feelings and emotion for a food or beverage product irrespective of consumer's ability to accurately articulate those feelings are needed in order to generate more accurate food and beverage product testing results. These methods will be based on the measurement of human physiology-most likely facial expressions, but they reveal intentionally hidden or subconscious emotions. In addition, the method may be able to decide emotions: Such as happiness, sadness, surprise, fear, anger feeling when one youth person eats a food or drinks beverage product. The first aspect main problem concerns how face reading technology can be measured to predict consumer acceptance level of confectionery foods or soft drinks from their face expression in the short time more absolutely. However, this face reading technology can't be used to predict any consumer's individual enjoyable acceptance satisfactory level when who uses any manufacturer's products in the short time.So face reading technology can not be used to predict any consumer's emotion to reflect to use any product more easily.

Thus, I shall recommend how to use video camera recording ethnographic research method to find what factors to influence the consumer who decides to buy the product to use and evaluate whose satisfactory level to use the product at home. I concern how to use video camera to predict consumer individual behavioral process to find why who choose to buy the kind of product to evaluate the most absolute emotion response to find whether who satisfies or doesn't satisfy to use the product. Also how to use face reading technology to measure different level sugar elements to add the confectionery foods to detect the consumer's emotion whether who likes or does not like to eat the kind of confectionery food.

- Summary of ethnographic research

of facial reading technology and video camera technology

To detect consumer's emotion like or not like to eat the confectionery foods, e.g. soft orange juice, sweet and chocolates. The food manufacturer may attempt to use face reading technology to predict different level sugar elements to add its confectionery eating products to see consumer's different face impression to evaluate whether what sugar elements , e.g. how much weights are the suitable level to add to the kind of confectionery food. To detect buyer's emotion whether who enjoy or does not enjoy to use the manufacturer's product and to find what factor(s)can influence the consumer to choose to buy the product. The home product manufacturer may use digital cameras and computer recording method to record the volunteer daily routines filmed at home. It aims to detect consumer's individual using behavior to research whether what psychological factors are to influence who to choose to buy themanufacturer's product to use. Otherwise, Ethnographic research concerns how to use video camera to record consumers' behavior daily about one weeks. It aims to predict what factors case who to buy the kind of product. Hence, Confectionery manufacturers can use face reading technology to predict consumer emotion of satisfactory level to eat sweats, ice creams, chocolates, biscuits etc. sugar add confectionery. Home product manufacturers can use video camera technology to predict consumer emotion of satisfactory level to use products at home e.g. clothing, radios, televisions, furniture, sleeping beds etc. home daily useful products.

- Comparative Benefits / Advantages

Face reading technology can help only confectionery eating food manufacturers to measure sugar element whether how much sugar weights are the most suitable to young people taste acceptable level more absolutely. Digital camera and computer recording technology can predict whether what factors can influence the consumer to choose to buy your competitor's similar product or your products and measure whose satisfactory level to let manufacturer to judge how to manufacture whose products of features are more suitable to be acceptable or attractive to consumers' taste.

If the confectionery eating food manufacturer could not detect consumers' emotion to know whether what level of sugar ingradient is the most suitable level to cause who are like or dislike to eat or drink confectionery foods from whose face expression absolutely. It will be serious loss to invest time and money to manufacture this foods and consumers will feel their foods or soft drinks is not health to eat to cause illness possibly. Traditional sensory and consumption tests predict consumer acceptance of new food products rather poorly, as are evidenced by the high their failure rates in the market. These tests typical reflect conscious processes whereas consumer acceptance may also be based on unconscious processes. For example, I feel functional (MFR) isn't an allowable technology space primarily due to consumer concern of manipulation. Miller (2012) indicated that " functional MRI mind reading technology is where something is wholly subjective and private, and it can't be predict consumer emotion to tell from what who're doing or looking at, what whose mental state is." Hence, It has a distinction between that kind of mind reading and what is brain reading, which essentially involves using brain scans to figure out what the factors can influence on consumer's mind in different situations to decide buy or not buy the food product. So, any consumer emotion researcher needs to wait a few seconds to see what consumers will do next. The technology is still limited, such as individual differences: Different consumers' brains code information sight differently, so consumer emotion researcher needs to learn how a specific individual codes consumers‘ emotion mental states. How to produce the most acceptable sugar level to manufacture any confectionery eating food or drink for children, it can keep consumers who will choose to buy other brands of confectionery eating food or drink more easily. This is the most important factor to influence your children taste choice to feel your brand confectionery eating food or drink is the best taste to compare other brand competitors. So, sugar ingradient (element) of the acceptable level is the most important research from face reading technology experiment in shop or factory.

The Netherlands (2014) indicated "Arnade had been carring to investigate consumers (man age 22 years) were recruited at the kaunas University of Technology. They were asked to rate the sample and then are characterized by Face reader program (Naldus Information Technology) Wageningen. The measurements are showed significant differences between facial expressions by the different samples of tested sugar element confectionery products and reflected liking ratings well. The positive correlations of facial expression happy and negative correlations of sad expression are predicted. It suggested that these may be the most valuable descriptors for explaining the quality of sweets and chocolates. It can be concluded that Noldus face reader technology is sufficiently accurate for differentiating between sugar confectionery products and can deliver additional information to conventional acceptance tests. " Otherwise, reasons for likes or dislikes of different foods or drinks are typically difficult to articulate, but may determine much of our food or drinks choice. Certain foods or drinks can be more active than other foods or drinks because for some reason who make consumers feel good when their express positive emotion. Arnade (2014) examined "consumers' facial reaction by the flavor of orange juice drinks using face reader technology measurement showed significant differences between facial expressions by the different samples. The explicit measurement reflected the liking ratings well. Especially expressions happy with liking and were good indicators for liked and liked samples respectively, 20 minimize artefacts, caused by the face reader software as emotion, they used liquid samples (juice) which need less processing in the mouth than solid samples." The aim of this work was to examine whether facial expressions measured with the Noldus face reader technology are a sufficiently accurate measure for differentiating between various types of sugar element confectionery including sweets, chocolates and juice drinks or soft drinks which need sugar element to add in the manufacturing processing and to investigate whether facial reactions are able to explain such these confectionery foods or drinks liking ratings.

The impact of emotions on judge , evaluations and decisions has long been important to psychology and consumer behavior on consumption. It seems face reading technology can predict whether the consumer likes or dislikes these confectionery foods, chocolates, sweets or juice, soft drinks liking ratings to measure whether sugar element is excess or less from young consumers‘ face expression, such as enjoying or not enjoying of feeling, smile or no smile response. Hence, face measuring technology can be more difficult to detect consumers 'emotion for product manufacturer. Because consumers need to spend more time to attempt to use their new innovative products.

- Recommendation Ethnographic consumer behavior research is for video camera recording to product manufacturers at home

Otherwise, it seems product manufacturers can't use face reading technology to detect consumers' emotion in the short time immediately. The products include any kind of products, e.g. high technological products, such as space mining of resources machines, satellite navigation system ,cars , machines etc. as well as home useful technological electronic products, such as mobile phones, washing machines, televisions, laptops as well as daily products, such as shirts, shoes, furniture, toys, tooth pastes etc. These essential home product and high technologic product manufacturers who need to continue to innovate their old style products to follow consumers' taste to invent new style products to be accepted to their fresh taste.

It seems that manufacturers need to spend a long time to touch consumers' feeling whether whose old style technological products which are still accepted to them to use or not. Hence, it implies that a consumer decides to buy these high technological innovation products, whose choice isn't performed to show who must accept to use these high technological innovation productsfor long time, whose emotion is not sure whether who feels satisfactory to consume to use this product for a long time. When he/she uses this technological product for a long time, it is possible that who will feel it was not valuable to buy it before. Hence, video camera can used to record the consumer's behavior record whose image and to analyze whose facial expressions and bodily gestures at home about one week.

- How to use video camera recording to predict consumer's emotion .

How to use automated facial expression analysis for emotion and behavior prediction. The expression of emotion is achieved through combinations of verbal and nonverbal information produced from various sources of the body and the brains. Nonverbal information encompasses any message that is not expressed in words, including gestures, postures to be performed from individual behavior for individual daily life. Though people often don't invest much thought to the nonverbal aspect of communication to be performed to manage emotional experiences. Computers enable researchers to process to gather data in a short amount of time to predict facial expression consumers. The new methodological for social scientists may be a valid analysis to automated facial expression from consumer's daily behavior at home experiement for several days investigation more absolutely. Among the various models of nonverbal communication, we focus on facial expression which are captured by small digital cameras and later analyzed with computer software.

As Webb et. al. (2000) pointed out, "people are low-fidelity observational instruments recording and interpretation may be erratic over time, as the observer learns and responds to the research phenomena he or she observes. It means that we can observe consumer behavior to predict why who buy the product from whose daily life behavior performance. Recent studies applied automated feature extraction and classification to extract macro features . Such as the head and hand position and angle from video features taken during an experiment where a theft took place. It also implied that computer models obtained up to 71 percent correct classification of innocent or guilty participants based on the macro features extracted from the video camera. Furthermore, in an overview of detection research." Meservy et al.(2008) noted that "the accuracy of humans coding behavioral indicators only falls around 50 percent, but that computers trained to a automatically extract and identify relevant behavioral cues detect deception with significantly higher accuracy. Furthermore, computers operate without the other methods(e.g. physiological measures such as polygraph machines or lie detectors) and the lost of extensively trained human interviewers."

Ambady and Rosenthal (1992) showed that "another advantage of why automated facial detection technology coupled with computational models is that once the system secures the parameters for a model, prediction of behavior (vs simple detection and classification) can be made using only a small sample. This is a computational recording of what social psychologists, a way people sample a short except from social behavior to draw inferences of about states, traits and other personally relevant characteristics .For instance, based on an observation of a three minute video clip of a conflict between a married couple."

Carrere and Gottman(1999) also indicated "video cameras were able to predict the outcome of that marriage after six years. Using machine learning coupled with computer vision allows computers to cause this human cognitive process; models are trained on a short sample of facial features and those features automatically predict future behaviors. Computers were used in place of human coders to detect vocal behaviors (e.g. time spent speaking, influence over conversation partners, variation in pitch and volume and behavior mirroring) during a negotiation task. Their results imply that the speech features extracted during the first five minutes of negotiation are highly predictive of future outcomes." The researchers also noted that using computers to code speech features offers advantages such as high test-retest reliability and real time feedback. As a cost-effective and relatively accurate method to detect, track and create models for behavior classification and prediction, automatic facial expression analysis has the potential to be applied to multiple disciplines. Capturing behavioral data from participants may be a more accurate representation of how and what they feel, and a better alternative to self-report questionnaires that interrupt participants' affective cognitive processes and are subject to bias .Our model goes beyond to predict the future behavior within a given task (e.g. a virtual car accident or an error in performance). This opens up the possibility of such models becoming a common methodology in social scientific and behavioral research.

Installing video camera recording at sample consumers to carry on investigating their feeling to use their product to collect the more truly acceptable or not acceptable feeling to use the product reason, such as: video camera recording method is data synchronization and time series statistics calculation. In the next phase of analysis, video recording are recording with data collected from experimental tasks such as surveys or simple motor tasks. This is done to map the extracted facial geometry information to behavioral output data. In the experiments three to five second intervals of facial expressions were taken one to two seconds before each instance of the behavior to be predicted and used as the input data. After data synchronization we also computed a series of time-domain statistics on coordinates in each interval to use as additional inputs to our classifiers. For example one sample investigating. The input data for this study consisted of videotapes of forty one participants watching films that elicited the emotions of either amusement or sadness, along with measures of their cardiovascular activity responding. It should be noted that the recorded expressions were expressions, unlike the photographs of deliberately posed faces often used in prior facial expression research. However, I suggest these entertainment product or home product manufacturers who can use video cameras to record whose buyers' behavior to detect whose emotion to aim to design which kind of colors, styles, sizes and how to change whose old products' features to attract the more consumers' fresh demand taste .

Ethnographic research is interpretative research which seeks an understanding from the perspectives of the value systems of those being researched. Ethnographic search is one different method to learn about buyer individual behavior to compare with enquiring questionnaires to participants to fill to answer questions to gather data to carry on the sale and post purchase evaluation cycle to evaluate whether what are their product criteria or weaknesses which need to improve to raise their sale competition in their market.

Palmer (2012) reported " one sport shoe company's ethnographic research in action was provided by a product commissioned by the footwear brand Dr Martens. It aims to research how to understand young people's buying behavior. It wanted to understand how youth people used brands in their every lives. Why for example, did some brands , such as Nike trainers or baseball caps become popular in youth culture? The researchers identified groups of young people around the world who responded to Dr Marten's target market. In return for a payment, volunteers were followed for several days and their daily routines filmed with a handheld digital camera. In total, 180 hours of captured film was edited to just one hour of highlights showing the key drivers of youth culture which are relevant to the Dr Martens brand. It seems that young people preferred fashions that allowed them to customize an item of clothing and in some way take ownership of it. The research drew the conclusion that iconic fashion items for young people had to have a distinctive label or style that made their wearers stand out as part of a tribe." Hence, ethnographic research seems to help this company to know why the young clients choose to buy those brands sport shoes, it is possible that the these brands sport shoes' color or design can be accepted more to them to buy Dr Marten brand's sport shoes when they wear different style of clothing. Hence, it uses digital cameras to observe the worldwide choice of paying target youth volunteers whose daily individual behaviors at homes to get the more actual evidence to evaluate what factors influence youth clients choose to buy these brands of sport shoes. It seems this sport shoe company can take several hours of filming to yield just a few moments of true insights to participant's true attitudes and behavior.

Ethnography is one of many approaches that can be found within Social research. Ethnography was a descriptive account of a commonly or culture. Ethnography usually involves the researcher participating in people's daily lives for an extended period of time, watching what happens, listening to what is said, and/or asking questions through informal and formal interviews collecting documents. In more detailed terms, ethnographic work usually has most of the following features: People actions are studied in every contexts rather than under conditions created by the researcher, in experimental or high structured interview situations as well as data are gathered for a range of sources including documentary evidence of various kinds, but participant observation and/or relatively informal conversations are main ones as well as data collected is for the most past relatively unstructured in two senses and it doesn't involve following through detailed research design at the start and the categories that are used for interpreting what people say or are not built into the data collection process through the use of observation schedules or questionnaires to analyze.

Generally, fairly small scale perhaps a style setting or group of people. This is a facilitate in depth study and analysis of data involves interpretation of the meaning, functions and consequences of human actions and low are implicated in local and perhaps also wider contexts what are produced for the most part are verbal descriptions, explaining and theories and statistical analysis play a subordinate role at most. How ethnography can learn more about buyer behavior to help product manufacturers to detect consumers' emotion. It means collection of data to pursue an answers to these questions more effectively and to test those against evidence. Hence, video camera recording to consumer's individual useful behavior at whose home. It isn't set up for research purposes (such as experiments or formal interviews).

The methodological model for social research is physical science conceived in terms of the logic of the experiment. However, ethnography was sometimes dismissed as quite inappropriate to social science on the grounds that data and findings it produces are subjective. Hence, ethnographic research is the role to learn more about buyer behavior through marketers may have been listening more to consumers (e.g. through qualitative research), efforts have almost always been directed at controlling consumers ranges of products or services predetermined by producers have been pushed through with littler real involvement of consumers in the process at a time in which consumers are ever more aware of what is being done to marketers. To seeing consumer's daily life behavior can predict why who choose to buy your or your competitor's product. Then, the product manufacturer can judge what the reasons are caused to attract the consumer chooses to buy the product to use. Hence, the data analysis procedure will include these steps as below:

- First step, Facial expression videos camera record activity ; input data from given tasks will be carrying on researching at the same time.
- Second step, the feature extraction will be caused
- Third step, the chi-square feature selection will be caused
- Fourth step, the machine learning training will be caused
- The final step, the results of behavioral prediction and data classification will be output at the same time.

- Why ethnographic research can be predicted consumer's behavioral performance to detect emotion by video recording camera at home ?

Ethnographic field research involved the study of groups and people as go about every day lives. There has two distinct activities. First the ethnographer enter into a social setting and gets to know the people and observes all the approach. But second the ethnographer writes down regular systematic ways what who observes and learns when participating in the quality rounds of life of others. Thus, the researcher creates an accumulating written records of these observations and experiences. Two interconnected activities comprise the care of ethnographic search: participation in some initially familiar social world and the production of written accounts of that world by drawing upon such participation. Hence, ethnographers are committed to get close to the activities and everyday people. Getting close minimally requires physical and social proximity to the daily rounds of people lives and activities, the field researcher must be able to take up positions in order observe and understand whom.

Consumer behavior refers to the behavior that consumers display in searching for purchasing , using , evaluating and disposing of products and services that who expect will satisfy their needs and it's behaviors that are directly involved in the action of obtaining, consuming and spending products or services, including the decision processes that precede and follow these actions. It seems ethnographic research can helps the marketer to understand how consumer think, feel and select from alternative like products, brands and the like and how the consumers' buying behaviors are influenced by their environment, the reference group, family and salespersons.

Consumer buying behavior includes that: Attitude itself is a learning experience and can lead to a change in attitude before buyers enter the buying process. Thus, attitude don't automatically guarantee all types of behavior. Attitudes based on behavioral learning follow beliefs, behaviors and effect sequence. A consumer who is high involved with a product or service category and who perceives a high level of product or service differentiation between alternatives with follow the cognitive hierarchy (belief affect behavior). From the ethnographic research marketers perspective the sequence of attitude formation is from a communication point of views from a strategic point of view, such as it has proved useful in specifying the different elements that work to influence buyers' evaluations of attitude, product or services may be composed of attributes or qualities, some of which may be more important than others to particular people. So consumer's individual decision is to act on whose attitudes is affected by other factors, such as whether it is felt other factors, such as whether it is felt that buying a product or service would be met with approval by friends and family.

According to this approach, ethnographic research marketers must concentrate an assessing the characteristics of the environment, such as the physical surroundings and product or service placement, that influence members of that target market. Such as point of purchase (such as selling the sport shoe brand's some sample of design style shoes) are particularly useful in predicting to find reasons why individual consumer choose to buy these styles. Hence, I recommend ethnographic research marketers can focus on measuring consumers' effective emotion response to products or services and develop offering that elicit appropriate subjective reactions and employ effective symbolism to predict how the different brand products to be designed which kind of style, to be used what kinds of colors and what kinds of materials to be produced.

To decide which is the most acceptance to satisfy consumers' taste. Such as the above sport shoe brand company case showed that it attempted to use ethnographic method to research whether what the external or internal factors are influenced to the footwear brand Dr martens' other consumers to choose the Nike or Baseball brands sport shoes to buy. It discovered that what youth people whose daily wearing clothing colors, designs and materials external factors which can influence them to choose to buy which kinds of design styles, colors and materials made of sport shoes to buy. It seems famous brands of sport shoes and cheaper price and durability internal factors are not the important factors to influence them to choose to buy these brands. Otherwise, the youth people whose wearing clothing colors, design styles and material made external factors can influence their feeling to choose the most adaptable style of sport shoes to be accepted to adapt to accept to their wearing clothing fashion. Thus, it seems that ethnographic research is one good method to detect consumers emotion whether the individual consumer's choice is influenced by the product's internal factors more or external environment external factors more to influence every individual consumer to feel positive or negative emotion to make final decision to buy any product to use possibly. If the product manufacturer can use this ethnographic research method to attempt to find whether what external or internal factors can influence potential consumers' fashion acceptance level to choose to buy any new innovative products to predict their emotion before the new peoduct manufacturer decides to manufacture its products to sell in this competitive market. I believe that its predicting market success chance will be increased.

Q3` What factor(s) can influence consumer chooses to buy any product or food in psychological view ?

The second aspect problem is judged whether constructive consumer choice is an important process to influence any consumer to choose to buy any products. If it is a real essential choice process, how product manufacturers can reduce their negative emotion is caused to choose not buy their products during this constructive process. The second aspect main problem is researched about consumer will choose to make final decision to buy the best choice of product from among brands of products . Hence, the constructive consumer choice process is a real essential choice process to any consumer generally, when individual consumer needs to compare different brands of products to choose to buy any product.

How product manufacturers can predict whose choice method to decide to prefer to make final decision to buy any products in the short days or the short time in the constructive consumer process. If manufacturers can know overall consumers' choice method, manufacturers will not design the not suitable style of products to manufacture to sell and who can know what the overall consumers' negative emotion is influenced who decide not to buy their products from their design style in order to manufacture more suitable style of product design . I shall recommend how manufacturers can predict consumer emotion in the constructive consumer choice process in psychological view.

My research is concerned knowledge opinion about how to predict consumer emotion whether what attribute factor(s)
are the most influence to the consumer to choose to buy the
manufacturer's product in whose process of choice. If manufacturer can early know whether what the most attractive attribute factor(s) are the most influence to the consumer to decide to buy whose product, so who can concentrate on manufacturing the different kinds of products to get the most influence attribute factor to attract consumers to choose to buy whose products. Hence, the manufacturer can know what reasons can cause the consumers who do not choose to buy its products during constructive consumer choice process generally , who can know how to improve its product's design method to concentrate on producing the most acceptable satisfactory level to sell to

whose consumers in .Also I believe that the manufacturer can raise sale numbers if who know what bad factors to cause whose consumers choose not to buy whose products during the constructive consumer choice process. It can increase chance to change its product innovative strategy to raise confidence to judge what attributed factors are the important influence to cause consumers who either do not choose to buy or choose to buy its innovative products.

The attributable factor of any product may include some or all these factors. For example: Safety, durability, reasonable price, fashion, pretty design, loyalty, etc. different factors whether which attributed factor can cause the consumer feels positive emotion to prefer to choose to buy the manufacturer's innovative products. I shall recommend how to predict consumers' positive emotion to the manufacturer's products in the consumer's constructive choice process. However, the benefits to manufacturers if who can predict what attribute factors have much influence consumers to make final decision in the constructive consumer choice process. It includes as below:

- Concentrate on manufacturing the new products to predict which attribute factors are the importance existed to influence consumers' whose final decision to choose to buy the manufacturer's any kind of products in order to raise chance to increase sale numbers.
- To let consumers have more confidence to choose to buy the manufacturer's any products to use for long time.
- Avoiding to spend excess money and resources and time to concentrating on manufacturing the new product which own much of not important attribute factors to influence consumers to choose not to buy the manufacturer's products .
- Market review of constructive consumer process research limit

I feel that constructive consumer choice process can only be predicted to find whether what attributable factors can influence the consumer to choose to buy the manufacturer's product from shopping retail market only, but it can't not predicted from online shopping.

Because consumer needs to spend more time to compare different similar brands of product to find what the attributable factor(s) own(s) to the brand of product to attract who to make the final buying decision. If the consumer choose to buy the product, usually, who won't spend more time to gather the similar products' information to decide to which kind of product and who will buy the product from internet immediately. Otherwise, if the consumer choose leave home to walk to different shops to choose to buy the kind of product, who have more time to spend to different shops to compare the different brand products to make final buying decision. Hence , constructive consumer choice process will only occur at visiting shops' consumption to any individual or group consumption.

- Related Background of constructive consumer process

May constructive consumer choice process is a psychological factor to influence consumers' emotion to make final decision to buy either kind of emotion product or rational product in consumption market generally. How can product manufacturers detect consumers' emotion to judge whether their products are belonged to be more kind of emotion product or rational product during they decide to sell different kind of products or foods to consumers?

Constructive consumer choice is an important process to influence any consumers to choose to buy any products. I shall give my idea to indicate how product manufacturers can predict whether their products are belonged to be either more kind of emotional product or more kind of rational product at different suitation. It aims to reduce their negative emotion is caused to choose not buy their products from their constructive consumer choice process.

Consumer decision making trends technological change and information explosion nowadays. Generally, consumers need to compare different brands of products from their characteristics , such as quality, fashion, design style, colors, prices, functions etc. factors to decide which is the most valuable choice to buy among of these different kinds of similar products from global consumption channel, such as electronic internet shopping channel or traditional retail shopping channel of two kinds of sale methods. Due to consumers can get any kinds of products' the most updated information from internet, television , magazines etc. advertisement channel at home conveniently. Thus, it causes nowadays consumers will concern to use a variety of strategic contingent on their consumption to demand to choose to buy what is the most valuable product considerately.

After consumers spend much time to make constructive choice, who will make final decision to choose to buy which kind of product is the most valuable from their positive emotion. In general, before any consumer chooses to make decision to buy any product, whose option is in a choice it will be assumed to have a utility or subjective value feeling to the product that it depends only on the option. Finally, it is assumed that the consumer has ability of skill in a computation that enables the calculation of which option will maximize whose received value and selects accordingly.

Why are preferences constructive logic buying decision in constructive consumer choice is important? One reason individuals may construct preferences is that who lacks the cognitive resources to generate well preferences for many situations. A second important reason is that consumers often multiple goals to be given decision problem. It implies preferences constructive choice will influence any consumer to change whose emotion to prefer to buy the product among of the same kind of target products. However, the fact that a choice is contingent need not simply that the processing was constructive , that is developed on the spot. A food or soft drink can be either a rational product or emotional product. For example, a consumer may have a well established, but contingent, preference for have chocolate on a cold day and a cold soft drink on a warm day, such a preference is not constructive to influence the consumer's emotion to spend long time to compare other similar foods or drinks to make the final decision to choose to buy the chocolate or a cold soft drink among of the other similar kind of target foods or drinks in supermarket. In this situation, it seems that the chocolate and soft drink is emotional product. A major purpose , therefore is to provide a conceptual framework for understanding constructive consumer choice how to influence consumers' emotion to make final consumption decision in the rational environment only. This framework then allows to accomplish the two major goals:

(i) Reviewing consumer decision research with the framework serving as a organizing device and (ii) Using this review to gaps in my knowledge that suggest new research directions to predict consumer's individual emotion of purchasing behavior. In general, in consumer view point, consumer product motive can provide two kinds of motives . One kind is emotional product motive which persuades the consumer on the basic of whose emotion, the buyer doesn't try to reason out or typically analysis the need for purchase. Another kind is rational product motive which arises on the basic of logical analysis and proper evaluation, the buyer makes rational decision after chief evaluation of the purpose, alternatives available, cost benefit and such valid reasons.

How to predict consumer decision tasks and decision strategies? In some cases, the two options may be simply to either accept or reject an alternative. The attributes may vary in consumers' potential consequences, the product desirability to the consumer and the consumer's acceptance to make off less of one attribute for more of another. For example, a consumer may fairly certain about the values of some of the attributes. (e.g. reliability, safety factors) to the product to influence the consumer's buying decisions. For example, a consumer considers the cars to decide that safety was the most important attribute, processed only that attribute with the best value on that attribute limited effectively requires selective attention to information or a consumer might engage in attribute processing by examining the price of each of the cars. Including that car (B) was the most expensive, car (A) was the least expensive, and that (C) had a very good price. However, the consumer could process in an alternative based fashion by examining the reliability, price, safety of car (A) in order to form a overall valuation of the car. In compensatory strategy, a good value on one attribute can't make up for a poor value on another. If a consumer decide to choose the safest car, then car(D) will be chosen regardless of as high price and regardless of the high ratings for car (B) on reliability or car (E) for fashion.

- Consumer decision strategies

First step, the amount of information processed. For example, an automobile choice is as implied by most rational choice models to consider each of the available cars or it may only a consideration of a limited set of information. (e.g. repeating what one choice last time). Second step, different amount, information can be processed for each attribute or alternative (selecting processing) or same amount of information can be processed each attribute or alternative. Third step, the pattern of processing (whether by alternative (brand) or by attribute. Final step, the consumer will select to buy the product, based on whether the strategy is compensatory or non compensatory.

In addition, aspects of the environment the capture involuntary attention may set in motion and consumer behavioral responses. (e.g. in a loud environment is as a threat to cause the consumer's negative emotion to decide to buy the product). It implies quiet environment has more positive influence to consumer's individual emotion. For many consumer choice, there is little emotion involvement or need to justify. The choice goals and the extent to which different strategies accomplish these goals in different task environment. For example, proposed measured of cognitive effort and accuracy. With respect to cognitive effort, any decision strategy can be decomposed into more elementary information processes, such as reading on item of information, comparing two items of information, eliminating items of information and so on for a general decision to analyze information processing for each individual consumer when who need to choose to buy any products. For another example, a consumer can conceptualize to read the value for each attribute weight, comparing the weight just read with the largest weight found previously until the most important attributable has been found and then reading the values for the options on that attribute and comparing the until the largest value is found. It weight adding strategy could be thought as reading weights and values, multiplying the two ,moving on to the next weight and value and multiplying them, adding the product.

Consumer sometimes face emotion choice. Such choices arise when there are choice conflicts between goals that are very important to the individual. (e.g. one can't attain all goals given the set of available options and must give up something on one important goal to attain more of another important goal). Examples of such emotion consumer choices include trading off the safety of an automobile against environmental concerns (if larger vehicles fare better in crashes but worse in gas mileage) or trading health risks due to the presence of insects in one's house versus health risks from having chemicals sprayed in one's yard. Such choice can easily lead to negative emotion, since the trade-offs required represent threats to the attainment of importance or valued goals. The degree of emotion often depends on the values of the options. (e.g. the degree of conflict and which specific attributes are involved in the conflict). However, the negative emotion is caused by the consumer's choice process, it is not only caused by external environment, e.g. noise influence. Choice processes under negative emotion may therefore be affected by accuracy and effort concerns as modified by emotion minimization concerns. In particular, two general copying strategies may apply in consumer emotion situations: problem focuses copying (direct actions aimed at improving the person environment relationship to influence the consumer's emotion), and emotion focused copying (indirect actions aimed at minimizing emotion through changes in the amount or content of thought about the situation). Hence, manufacture will expect that increased negative emotion due to the choice situation will lead to more extensive processing. New products were evaluated more favorably when their attributes were moderate only when consumers had limited knowledge about the product category.

Consumers had more extensive knowledge about the category , their evaluations were influenced by associations to specific attributes based on their final choice level. Thus, knowing what the consumer's the most need of attributes of the product is very important in whose construct choice process. The affective tests consumer emotion's prediction weakness. The primary purpose of affective tests is to assess the personal response (preference or acceptance) of current or potential customers to a product idea or a specific product characteristics. Qualitative affective tests are those (e.g. interviews and focus groups) that measure subjective response of a sample of consumers to the sample kinds of products by having those consumers talk about their feelings in an interview or small group setting. A highly trained interviewer/ moderator is required because of the high level of interaction between the interviewer/ moderator and the consumers. Types of qualitative affective tests include focus groups, focus panels, mini-group and one-on-one interviews. However, qualitative affective tests will have these problems, such as with focus groups, individual answer can get lost in the group conversation. In addition, individual can reject from expressing opinions contrary to the group because of perceived peer pressure or group think. Panels which are focus group that meet repeated suffer from the same problems as focus groups. With one-on-one interview fasters might substantially temper a negative assessment of a product in order to not to appear honest answer or because they like the interviewer and don't want to hurt their feelings.

● Internet questionnaires recommendation

I recommend any individual company can send internet questionnaires to individual to detect what attribute factors

can influence individual consumer's emotion to make the final consumption decision to choose to buy its innovative new products by email before their new products will be manufactured. Thus, the manufacturer can predict whether what attribute factor can be the most potential influence to individual's emotion to choose to buy whose new products generally. For example, one car manufacturer can send email questionnaires to individual consumer to invite who to fill its questionnaires in its website, these questionnaire questions can indicate as below:
(a) What attribute factor(s) can influence you to choose to buy our company's new design style sport car products?. reliability .new fashion .fast speed .brand .popular. reasonable price . durability, .safety .more functions . unique design style
(b) Which factor do you feel which is the most important to influence you to make the final buying decision to choose to buy our company's new design style sport car products ?
In general, this company's all sport cars which are rational products. It means any consumer will prefer to spend time to compare its any style of sport cars to other brands of sport cars to make final decision to choose to buy which brand of sport car. For example, if one consumer feels safety attribute factor is the most important to influence who chooses to buy any sport cars. Then, he/she will demand to attempt to drive to detect this car company's any style of sport cars to test whether which can satisfy to whose safe demand. Even, if who feel other brands' style of sport cars can satisfy whose safe demand, he/she will be possible to attempt to drive to detect other brands of similar style sports cars to compare to this brand of sport car to make final purchase decision.
Owing to there are many brands of sport cars which are provided to individual consumer to compare to choose to make final decision to buy in any country. It seems that any consumer will prefer to spend time to make logical and rational analysis to compare them and who won't be influenced by whose emotion to decide to buy any brands of sport cars in the short time easily. Thus sport cars is belonged to rational product more then emotional product.
As this reason, so I recommend this sport car company needs to prepare email questionnaires to enquire its potential individual consumer to attempt to let who to give feedback to predict whether what attribute factors can influence whose emotion to choose to buy its any kind style sport cars as well as whether what attribute factor will be the most importance to compare the other attribute factors to make final cause to influence final decision to choose to buy its any sport cars to avoid the worst attribute factor is caused. Following the car company gathers different feedback to predict whether what attribute factors are as well as what the worst factor is from these sample potential consumer's idea of its email questionnaire. Then, it can predict the result from consumers' idea to make final decision whether which are the least attractive attribute factors which will influenced any individual consumer to decide not to buy its any style of sport cars.
It aims to predict whether what are the least attractive attribute factors to cause bad emotion to the consumer to choose not to buy the kind of sport car generally. Such as, not reliable engines, old fashion , slow speed, unpopular brand, not reasonable price, not durability, not safety, less functions or not unique design style of whether which are the least attractive attribute factors. Hence, it can predict whether which attribute factors will be the attractive influence to cause its any potential consumer to choose to buy its any new innovative sport cars in order to

concentrate on manufacturing any new innovative style sport cars to design which must own the most attractive attribute factors before it decides to manufacture its new style of sport cars. In conclusion, it seems that constructive consumer choice is an important process to influence any consumer to choose to buy any products. I recommend any company ought attempt to prepare questionnaires to investigate whether which the most attractive attribute factors are and which the least attractive attribute factors are influenced to each potential consumer will choose to buy or not buy to its launch innovative new products by email questionnaire channel. In general, youth people will feel ease to use online to shopping to compare to old people. I shall indicate online car brands comparison Constructive consumer choice processes

Table 1 An example of a consumer decision task

car reliability price safety speed

A worst best good very poor

B best worst worst good

C poor very good average average

D average poor best worst

E worse very good good best

Attributes are scored on seven point scales ranging from best to worst, with indicating the most desirable value for the attribute and worst indicating the least desirable value.

Q4 Is online sale (ecommerce) method the best channel to sell products nowadays ?

The third aspect solution, I shall explain why the electronic commerce sale channel in technology acceptance model, it is possible that why it can influence the consumer's positive emotion to be changed to be negative emotion to choose not to buy the manufacturer's product . Moreover, I shall teach manufacturer whether how to judge it ought or does not ought choose this technology model to sell its products from internet channel.

The third aspect main problem is researched why internet sale will have what bad factors to influence consumers to cause negative emotion to decide not to buy manufacturers' products from online shopping. I shall recommend how to predict their products whether which are suitable to sell from internet and how to improve their sale methods to increase consumer's positive emotion to accept to buy their products from internet. The final discussion is judged in what situation it will cause individual consumer doesn't like to enter the manufacturer's website to choose to buy the manufacturer's products.

I shall also indicate why the manufacturer will cause negative emotion to whose consumers if who chose online sale channel. I aim to teach manufacturer how to know whether whose products ought or not ought to be chose to sell from online sale channel as well as how to reduce to cause bad influence to consumers' emotion from whose websites to avoid online sale failure chance. I shall use internet surveys to gather information to detect whether what factors influence the consumer choose prefer to buy or not to prefer buy the manufacturer's products from internet as well as how manufacturers can predict consumer's emotion in the constructive consumer choice process before who choose online shopping. Hence, if the manufacturer could predict whether what weaknesses are existed to reduce whose website attraction to whose consumers' attention. It will avoid whose online sale failure. The benefits to manufacturer include who can predict what weaknesses of whose website are, then who can attempt to revise which aspects of whose website weaknesses in order to raise whose consumers' positive emotion when who uses internet to enter the sale website to find any kinds of products to buy them. If the manufacturer's website can raise attraction ability to increase many customers to see whose website. Then, whose customer numbers will be increased possibly. Online sale influence research can only apply to manufacturers who sell their products from their website sale channel.

- Related Background of internet sale channel

Nowadays, many young people like to choose to use internet to buy any manufacturer's products. Although internet is popular to accept to young to use to buy any products, but it will have chance to cause negative emotion to individual consumers from positive emotion due to they enter any manufacturer's website to find some bad points to influence their feeling to be bad. Finally, the consumers will not choose to buy the manufacturer's products due to the manufacturer does not know what the bad points are existed to whose website. Thus, I believe that internet won't be accepted to be the best sale channel to adopt to use to sell to any manufacturers' products effectively, even internet sale channel will cause some consumers negative emotion to influence who choose not to buy the manufacturer's products if the product's manufacturer chooses internet to help who to advertise whose this product to sell from internet sale channel.

Previous research has linked the experience of loneliness with materialism, suggesting that when consumers attach too great an importance to possessions, they may reduce the importance of their social relationships, leading to isolation and feelings of loneliness. Thus materialism may arises a way to cope with loneliness, which suggests that to decrease materialism, one may want to first focus on building social relationships and reducing loneliness rather than focusing first upon reduced consumption.

Hung & Mukhopadhyay (2012) examined the influence of actor versus observes perspectives on the emotional experience. "They find that "actors tend to focus move on the situation at hand and experience more emotion, such as excitement, sadness when who recall or anticipate emotional experiences. Their previous research has linked experiences of loneliness with materialism, suggesting that when consumers attach to great an importance of their social relationship, leading to isolation and feelings loneliness. This may unfortunately, lead to downward, thus it focus on building social relationship and reducing loneliness rather than focusing first upon reduced consumption." It seems social environment can influence the consumer's social emotion to choose to consume the product. The meaning of happiness that is most relevant to influence choices, such select those with a present focus will prefer products that offer calm. Thus, it seems excited consumers will choose exciting products and calm consumers will choose relaxing products. It implies that who will prefer to choose to buy the kind of product from online shopping if the consumer is a excited person to accept new technology shopping model and enjoyed to loneliness to sit down to use whose laptop to choose to buy any online products at home quiet environment. Otherwise, if consumers don't like loneliness, who will like to leave their homes to go to retail shops to buy any manufacturers' new innovate products with their friends or families and who will feel more happy and enjoyable in this non technological shopping model. Thus, it implies the enjoyable quiet environment, loneliness, technology excited consumers will choose to buy products from online sale model more. Otherwise, the enjoyable noise environment, social relationship, calm consumers will choose to buy products from traditional retail shops sale channel. Thus, consumers' emotion will be influenced to feel enjoyable or non-enjoyable to buy the product from the online shopping model or traditional visiting retail shops model .It seems that noise or quiet shopping environment will influence individual consumer's emotion to make final decision to buy the product. If the consumer enjoys to choose to buy any brands of products in the quiet environment at home lonely, the online shopping technological model will be more chance to be accepted to make final decision to this consumer habitually. Otherwise, if the consumer enjoys to choose to buy any brands of products in the noise environment, social relationship with friends, the visiting retail shops model will be more chance to be accepted to make final decision to this consumer habitually.

What is this meaning to this consumer in these two different situation? I feel that the consumer will prefer to choose to buy the kind of product from online shopping if who is a excited person, so who can accept to use internet more than visiting retail shops , due to who enjoys to loneliness to sit down to use whose laptop to choose to buy any online products at home quiet environment. Otherwise, if the consumer does not like loneliness, who will like to leave whose home to visit retail shops to choose to buy any brands of products with whose friends or families in the noise shopping center environment, due to who will feel more happy and enjoyable to buy any products in the noise and social relationship with friends or family outside environment. It means that the product manufacturer needs to understand whether whose products can be more accepted to sell to its potential consumers from either online sale model or visiting retail shops traditional sale model as well as how to design its product styles to match its potential consumers to build positive emotion whether this product is suitable to sell from online sale channel. In general, the perceived case of use can influence perceived usefulness of the product, then to influence consumer's attitude to choose to buy the product. Hence, attitude can influence the consumer's commonly. I feel that the consumer will choose to visit retail shops to test the product's functions or attempt to touch the product or see the product's actual image in the retail shops, even who needs the salespeople to teach who how to use the product when feel the product is difficult to learn to use. Specially, it is a new innovative technological product, when it will be promoted to market to sell in the first time. Due to the consumer did not know this new product existed before, who needs the salespeople talk to whom to explain how to use this new technological innovative product to listen carefully. So, who will choose to visit retail shops to decide to buy this product with whose friends or families more than online shopping. Otherwise, if the consumer feels the product is ease to use and who like loneliness, who will accept to use internet to make final decision to choose online to buy the product in the quiet home environment more than traditional visiting retail shops model. It seems the external environment and the consumer's personality can influence the consumer's emotion to make final decision to choose to buy any brand of product. For example, the consumer feels the product is ease to learn to use or difficult to learn to use. It will influence the consumer choose to buy either from online or retail shops.

- How can internet cause positive emotion to consumers?

Online shopping lacks emotion physically experienced (e.g. examined, tried on, and used), it is difficultly for shoppers with little computer expertise, there are some general uncertainties associated in homes hopping of all kinds (e.g. concerns about product return, credit card security, loss of privacy, merchant legitimacy.) Each consumer's confidence might play an important role in predicting intentions to purchase. The factors influence whose confidence which may include, such as consumer's lower perceived risk, product appearance, image size and product movement were manipulated in context of simulated appeal web sites. Both manipulations in the computer medicated environment were expected to create virtual experiences affecting mood, perceived risk and purchase intent product image size is a significant factor.

Product presentations using movement attract attention and generate good mood in on-line shoppers, even soft music listening in quiet home environment can influence consumer's emotion to cause online shopping intention. The benefits of online shopping in relation to traditional stores hopping are one of the driving forces in the adoption. Perceived usefulness has been used to explain consumer acceptance of online shopping. Perceived usefulness refers to the degree to which a person believes that using a particular system (e.g. an online shopping site) would enhance his or her job performance. Risk perception of online shopping can be risked into two predominant types behavioral risk and environment risk. Behavioral risk arises from online retailers who have a chance to behave in an opportunistic manner by taking advantage of the government's inability to monitor all transactions adequately.

It includes product risks, psychology risks and seller performance risks. Environment risk is caused by the unpredictable nature of the purchasing medium-internet, which is beyond the control of online retailer and consumer. It includes financial risks and privacy risks. Perceived risk can be affected or moderated by a variety of factors, including consumer demographics, internet experience, product characteristics and attributes of a web site etc.

The perceived product risk varies with the age and internet experience of consumers. As consumers get older, their accumulated experience and knowledge make their stopping more targeted of certain brands and make them more confident, which can reduce product risk and the need for conducting pre-product information searches. It is possible that in comparison to make consumers female consumers perceived the likelihood and consequences of negative outcomes as a result of purchasing online to be greater and their concerns regarding these verity of the consequences of privacy loss during online shopping were stronger. The effect of perceived risk may be subject to product characteristics. The risk is generally higher for high involvement products that require the problem solving behavior and have some degree of personal importance than for low involvement products. Hence, online retailers of low involvement products may have greater success in keeping buyers than those of high involvement products, if the former can provide on appealing shopping experience. Other attributes of products do matter to perceived risk .

For example, the risk was perceived lower for product for categories associated with higher expenditure levels, more satisfying characteristics and feeling and touching before purchase.

Consumer attitude is directly affected by users' belief about a system, which consist of perceived usefulness and once of use to use online to shopping in technology acceptance model to each individual consumer. In the technological acceptance model aspect view, it is possible that the consumer's perception of technology of safety and cost is important to influence who to choose to buy the product as well as self efficiency has been found to affect technology usage also through its effects on the emotional state of the user buy, for example, the manufacturer can reduce the consumer whose computer anxiety and it can increase behavioral control to its consumer more easily when its consumers enter it's product website to feel it is more safe to buy its products to compare to its online competitors' websites. Due to the characteristics of online retail context to innovative products, consumers are subjected to more influences in the virtual store where who are able to interact with an adaptive environment as a consequence on adaptive and interactive scenario is more appealing for consumers, with benefits for the decision making process. Thus, internet will influence consumers whose emotion to choose another online shopping model to any innovative products sale channel. Enjoyment can be considered the degree to which consumer perceives a certain technology as pleasant. It implies that richer technology leads to higher enjoyment for achieving a stronger influence on consumers' attitudes toward online retailers.

I shall recommend any one innovative product manufacturer ought send questionnaires by to any individual consumer by email to enquire about such as below:

(i) Do you feel this kind of innovative product is either easy or difficult more to learn to use ? It aims to predict their emotion to give feedback to let who to know whether consumers' emotion will be felt more easy or more difficult to use this product from these sample population. Then , this manufacturer can judge whether it ought to sell this kind of innovative product from either traditional retail shops or online shopping model.

(ii) Do you feel you like to buy this product in either quiet environment or noise environment more? It aims to predict their positive emotion response to judge whether who accept to buy this kinds of innovative product in the quiet environment or noise environment more to decide to make visiting retail stores channel or online sale online to sell this product.

(iii) Do you like to use internet advertisement or magazine advertisement channel to find this kind of product? It aims to predict internet online sale model or retail stores sale channel which is more acceptable to sell the manufacturer's products to attract to influence many customers to make final decision to buy its products more popular and acceptable.

(iv) Do you need salespeople to talk to you to give truly products information to assist you to buy my brand of any products? .absolutely need .absolutely not need .may be need. may not be need. It aims to judge whether the online sale is more important sale channel or not to compare with retail shops sale channel. After it gathers these statistic information from these sample potential Consumers' email questionnaires, the manufacturer can analyze whether this kind of innovate product is more acceptable from online sale model or traditional retail shopping model in its country, even global sale. Thus, it can decide either to increase to open more retail shops or decrease retail shops numbers or concentrating on selling its products from online sale channel more sale methods.

Summary

Consumer emotion prediction can have many methods. However, I feel that these three methods are the most useful. Firstly, video camera recording technology can predict why the consumer chooses to buy the kind of product as well as face reading technology can measure whether what weights of the sugar ingredients to manufacture the weight of sweets, chocolate, soft drinks of the most good taste foods. Secondly, the manufacturer can concentrate on manufacturing whose new product which can own the most attractive attributable factor to attract which customers to choose to buy to reduce the invent lose risk. Thirdly, website sale channel must not be suitable to any manufacturers to choose to sell which products. If who can know whether their products are suitable to sell from internet or retail stores sale channel more. It can reduce the risk to loss their customers in long time. However, if you feel your product or food ought to sell from online channel. I recommend you ought need to do marketing research to evaluate whether which sale channel is the most suitable to research to sell your products or foods to persuade your clients to choose to buy. Otherwise, if your online sale channel is not suitable to sell to cause bad emotion to your clients. Thus, I believe it will reduce your client numbers due to you sell your products in the wrong sale channel.

References

Ambady, N. and Rosenthal, R.(1992)' Thin Silces Of Behavior As Predictors Of Interpersonal Consequences: A meta- analysis, psychological Bulletin, 2: 256-74

Arnade, E. (2014) Journal Of Consumer Research, Make a face: Implict and explict measurement of facial expression by orange juices using face reading technology. Food quality and preference, vol.32, p.161-172. Retrieved: http://hdl.handle.net/10919/54538.

Carrere, S. and Gottman, J. (1999) ' predicting divorce amongnewlyweds from the first three minutes of a marital conflice discussion', family processes 38:293-301.

Hung & Mukhopadhyay.(June 2012), Emotion And Consumer Behavior, , vol. 40 no.5 (June 2012), 39-50.

Meservy, T.O. jnsen, M.L. Kruse, W.J., Burgoo, J.K. and Nunamaker Jr., J.F. (2008) ' Automatic extraction of deceptive behavioral cues from video', in H.Chen, E.

Reid, J. Sinai, A. Silke and B. Ganor (eds) Terrorism Informatics (pp. 495-516), New York: Springer.

Miller, K. (2012), Consumer behavior, Washington, USA. Retrieved: http://www.amazon.com

Palmer (2012), Consumer behavior and credit card payment, Journal of management market resarch.

Webb et. al (2000), The impact of perceived corporate social responsibility on consumer behavior, Journal of business research 59(1): pp. 46-53 Jan. 2006.

Q5 How terrorism attack influences traveller need ?

Nowaday, airline industry is entering global competition. So, any some less positive or negative social environment changing which will influence any airlines' passenger behavioral consumption change. For example, air ticket price rises or fuel price rises or the country's season is bad or the global economy is bad or the country has terrible death threat etc. different negative social environment change fastors which will influence any country passenger individual travel consumption desires.

In Special, business class airline transportation demands are also increasing, due to many business travelers need to catch planes to go to any different countries to do business as well as many cargoes need to be carried from planes to transport to different countries to sell. So, business class traveler target group behavioral consumption is difficult to influence travelling consumotion desires from external environmental factors because business class traveler target group concerns to need to catch planes to go to another country to discuss business co-operation with the country's businessmen. So, their business travel desires won't easy to be influenced more than individual entertainment travel consumer's desire.

It seems cargo and business aim of aviation transportation industry has less chance to be influenced to reduce businessmen traveler or cargo transportation numbers to compare to entertainment traveler numbers by external environment change influences, due to the business travelers and cargo transportation travelling desires is difficult to reduce travelling or transportation needs to reduce the " doing businesses to earn profit chance with another country's businessmen". However, ignorance of internal or external market dynamics, catching entertainment travelers business can be detrimental to airline profitability more than carrying cargoes or business travelers business. Because the demands of travelling different countries‘ travelers' consumption are still more than the demands of businessmen carrying cargoes in any countries every year. So, the global GDP of travelling income sector is still have the important position to any country nowadays.

How can positive or negative social environment change influence any airlines‘ air ticket prices to be risen or fallen as well as how can these social environment change influence passenger consumption desires ? For example: What is the petroleum price change influence ?In fact, the increase in petroleum price can have chance to affect every airlines passenger has a negative manner to reduce travel consumption because increased oil prices have resulted in the reduction of airline services operations, the number of airline schedules flights, even airline bankruptcies. Whether global economic inflation or deflation, terrorism threats to the country, oil shortage or oil price rising or fallening, bank interest rate increasing or decreasing etc. external factors which have the most influential causes to bring the bad or good effects to cause airline industry share price reducing or increasing or increasing or reducing air ticket price. In result, these external environmental changes will influence the global traveler numbers to be increased or decreased at the time.

To support this hypotheses, this are my research first question, such as : Does a combination of terrorism and price of petroleum significantly influence airline profit changing mostly? The alternative hypothesis was my research second question, such as: Whether a significant relationship exists between terrorism, price of petroleum and airline profitability more than other factors, such as inflation, bank interest rate or air ticket price changing of these factors to influence passenger consumption desires change. I shall indicate that the first assumption was that terrorism has a negative effect on airline profitability and another assumption was that only external factors as oil prices or terrorism affect airline profitability. Finally, the terrorism and oil shortage and oil rising price factors can influence every passenger travel consumption desire to be reduced mainly.

Terrorism attack influences traveller need

However the effects of oil price and terrorism on airline profitability was limited to a regional perspective, so oil price and terrorism external environmental change will only influence some countries' airline traveler numbers to be decreased, e.g. the terrorism attack of plane crash event to USA on 11 Sept. After the terrorism attack happened on USA 11 Sept. incident of terrorism attack was restricted to events of skyjacking, attacks on oil production, refinery and distribution. Then, due oil shortage will be caused due to reducing oil production, refinery and distribution as well as it will influence oil price is risen and airline ticket price is also risen. It will reduce travel consumption desire to some countries if their airlines' ticket prices are also increasing. Other types of terrorist activities, such as attacks on financial targets or senior government officials could have an adverse effect on the petroleum and airline industry. I think the disruption of the production or distribution of petroleum because of incidents of terrorism was costly in terms of loss of business and the inflationary effect on fuel dependent products or services.

In fact, some airlines have adopted more fuel saving technology, so whose fuel consumption would not use more than other non fuel saving technology airlines. It seems fuel price increasing will not be the only factor to influence the airline industry's traveler numbers decreasing due, the owning more fuel saving technologic airlines which air tickets prices won't influence to be risen , due to reducing oil production and shortage influences . However, due to some airlines which have fuel saving technology, so which can avoid to use more fuel to provide planes to use and which fuel costs will be reduced, then which can provide cheaper air ticket fare prices to compare the non fuel saving technology airlines. The result will cause some not owning fuel saving technological airlines which will lose travelling customers in this global airline travelling market, also the not fuel saving technological airlines need to renew their fuel technology if which want to keep their competitive abilities to avoid to close down their businesses. So, what factors will influence the not owning fuel saving technological airlines profitability to be reduce if the oil shortage factor can not influence their planes energy supply to be reduced to cause air ticket prices to be increased? To answer this question, I shall indicate another financial risk factor how it influences airline industry behavioral change.

Also, I shall indicate the financial risk of airline industry evidence from Cathay Pacific airways and China airlines against key determinants of which include interest rate, exchange rate and fuel price risk for the period of January 1996 year to December 2011 year. During this period, these key external factors which were the most serious influence to cause these two airlines choose to change their strategic behaviors. Due to any these financial risks is difficult to predict and it was also changing often, these factors will also affect any airlines stock returns which arise from changing economic conditions, e.g. fuel price movements and fluctuations in exchange rates. These external unpredicted changing factors will attribute to the air tickets cyclical demand, capital investment, fixed costs of labor and landing rights to this global airline industry. Finally, it will cause some airlines need to rise air ticket prices to reduce expenditures increasing.

However, the relationship between fuel price and stock prices varies across economies which will influence travel passenger consumption of desires. For example, the effects of oil price changes in sub-sector indices, such as wood, paper and printing, insurance and electricity. In the past, on global stock exchange market was positively significant in 2011 year. Otherwise, with respect to the U.S.A. aviation industry, some economists suggested that global airlines stock returns were negatively to percentage change in fuel prices related to any airline firm value, e.g. Qantas and Air New Zealand were negatively share price growth to fuel price risk in the short term in the 2011 year. Thus, due to these two airlines share price went down, it will influence investors who loss confidence to buy their shares as well as it will influence travelling passengers who choose to buy other airlines' air tickets to go to travel because they will feel these two airlines have business challenges, e.g. bad service quality and food quality and uncomfortable airline seat environment and poor management style. etc different bad feeling. So, these two airlines' share prices went down, it will influence every travel passenger's confidence to choose to buy their air tickets to sit their planes to go to travel.

Q6 Why MTR underground train transportation needs to know passenger behaviour ?

Understanding individual passenger behaviour is essential for the design MTR transportation, because who can choose to catch bus, taxi, tram, train ferry etc. different kinds of public transportation tools. Individual traveler who decides to catch which kinds of public transportation tools, it depends on whether the public transportation tool can provide real time travel information, liking link travel time schedule. So, MTR underground train needs to understand where it has terminal to give convenience to the local living areas of time travelers to choose to catch MTR easily. Although, MTR ticket fare is one factor to influence any passengers choice. But, those other factors can also influence them to choice. e.g. MTR any terminal location of convenience, short time travelling, none crowding in busy (peak) time, MTR platform waiting arrival time, none sudden MTR engineering machines broken accident events occurrence frequently etc. different factors, any one of these factors which can influence passengers who choose to catch MTR or other kinds of transportation tools.

- Why route choice can influence passenger behavioural choice

Usually, the busy time passengers will regard the route choice as a coordination problem to influence them to choose to catch which kinds of transportation tools. The route choice is as an opportunity costs to influence any busy time passengers to decide to choose to catch which kind of transportation tool which is the best right choice in the right time among of them. In the short time, for example, it seems any busy time passengers will choose to catch bus to substitute MTR underground train transportation tool, due to who feels the bus can arrive any destinations to compare other kinds of transportation tools in the most short time. However even if the MTR can either charge cheaper ticket fare to sell full day or charge discount ticket fare to sell in the busy (peak) time to compare to bus fare. It is possible that the busy time passengers will still choose to catch bus, if between the bus terminal and the another bus terminal that distance is the shorter time route to spend time to arrive destination to compare between the MTR terminal to the another MTR terminal arrival time . Also, although the busy time passengers will feel to enounter traffic jam to influence sitting or waiting bus time to be longer time in possible and who also feel MTR can avoid traffic jam problem. However, usually any busy (peak) time passengers will feel the chance of traffic jam occurrence will be less. So, the short bus route choice is more potential factor to influence the busy (peak) time passengers still to choose bus to catch.

However, if anyone wants to investigate results of day-to-day route choice which can be transferred to more realistic environment. It is necessary to explore individual behaviour in an interactive experimental set up to ensure busy (peak) time passenger transportation behavioural choice. For example, a passenger has a choice between a main road (M) and a side road (S) for travelling from (A) to (B). (M) is faster if (M) and (S) are chose by the same number of passengers. So, this method can be researched whether MTR terminal station is located at the main road (M) or the side road (S) where is more suitable to accept to passengers generally.

Q7 Why trip time reliability and crowding factors can influence MTR passenger choice?

Other problem is MTR busy (peak) time's crowding in public transportation occurrence of MTR underground train transportation tool is becoming a growth to concern as MTR demand growth at a busy (peak) time. To capture the MTR passengers benefits with reduced crowding from improved MTR public transport service and image. It is necessary a identify the relevant dimensions of crowding that are meaningful measures of what crowding means to MTR passengers. Two main influences on MTR model choice that are growing in relevance are trip time reliability and crowding. It represents a benefit-cost framework. In fact, MTR passengers can be willing to pay more expensive ticket fare, it MTR can avoid crowding and short and the accurate arrival trip time between terminals is reliable to occur. How to measure of MTR crowding, e.g. weighting the gap between the busy time, the standard (i.e. objective) and the perceived (i.e. subjective) metrics. We are not in a position to definitely map the two dimensions, which is a crucial requirement for translating objective improvements into equivalent subjective gains that then can be applied, willingness to pay estimates MTR ticket fares to obtain the additional MTR passenger benefits of MTR public transportation investment to any terminal stations. Because MTR crowding has a negative impact on passengers in terms of psychological on emotional distress. MTR passengers are willing to stand for up to 20 minutes of the service is fast and reliable. However crowding outweighed these benefits from a MTR passenger's perpective, experienced crowding leads a increased dissatisfaction. e.g. stress and less privacy during who needs to stand up in MTR. Due to there are no enough places to supply to them to stand up in MTR. If the MTR trip time was longer time between the passenger's terminals, who will feel more dissatisfaction and it will cause who feels whether who ought need to choose to catch other transportation tools to substitute MTR next time. e.g. bus, train, tram, ferry, taxi etc. So, from an operator's perspective, the MTR service frequency or MTR size is significantly influenced by the level of ridership, which sends a signal to respond if the monitored crowding level exceeds the benchmark standard in the busy time. e.g. in the morning time or at the night time, the students or employment people who need to go to schools or offices (working places). The locations of different places between MTR terminals and crowding are regarded as a key service attribute for MTR pubic transportation along with other factors, such as travelling time and reliability, e.g. service quality, none engineering machines are broken to cause MTR stops suddenly.

Given the increasing importance of crowding on both the disutility to existing MTR public transportation users and the influence to it. MTR passenger can choose to use either the MTR public public transportation or other public transportation. It is timely to review the MTR current measures of crowding defined by transportation authorities. MTR operators ought evaluate whether they apporpriately reflect MTR each traveler experiences and perceptions of crowding in busy (peak) time. I suggest that MTR needs to buy other underground trains to supply to the busy (peak) time passengers to let them have enough seats to sit down, so who do not need to stand up in any MTR underground trains when they catch MTR underground trains in busy time. It aims to let who are willingness to pay the estimation of reasonable ticket fares to compare the other kinds of transportation tools in the busy (peak) time.

Q8 What is the crowding difference between train and MTR underground train?
In fact, crowding won't be happened to brother these transportation tools easily in the busy time and non busy time both. e.g. bus, taxi, train, tram, ferry. Because passengers can not choose to stand up in these transportation tools easily, due to these transportation tools have no enough areas (spaces) to let them to stand up easily . So, the crowding will be avoided to occur in these tranportation tools usually. Otherwise, MTR will have many passengers who can choose to stand up because MTR design of length is very long and it has enough areas (places) to let passengers to choose to stand up, even there have none any seats are provided to let them to sit down. So, MTR passengers will feel more dissatisfaction and crowding easily, especial in any peak (busy) time every day.

Comparing to bus, much more diverse crowding measures are defined in the passenger rail industry. For passenger, different specifications for measuring crowding are found across countries and even within a country. For example, rail crowding measures in the UK, the passengers in excess of capacity is crowding measure that applies to all London and South east operators weekday train services at a London terminus during the morning peak from 0700 to 09: 59 , and those departing during the afternoon peak from 16:00 to 18:59 (office of rail regulation 2011 year). The overall PIXC figure is considered the planned standard class capacity of each train service as well as the actual number of standard class passengers on the service at the critical point. i.e. the location on a trains of standard class passengers that surpass the planned capacity as the difference between the number of actual passengers and the capacity of the train divided by the number of passenger is within the capacity . So, it seems train and MTR underground public transportaton tools had been encountering the crowding problems in peak time, the difference in train passengers need to wait next train or more train arrival is who doesn't plan to enter the train, when who discovers the current train has no seats to provide to them to sit down in whose trip. Otherwise, MTR passengers can choose either to stand up within the large areas (places) if who discovered there are no any seats to provide to them to sit down or who can wait the next MTR arrival in order to who can sit down. It seems MTR transportation tool crowding environment includes in waiting platform and inside of the MTR underground train. Otherwise, train transportation tool crowding environment only includes the waiting platform and the passengers will not have crowding feeling inside of the train, due to none of passengers choose to stand up inside any trains because any train inside has no enough places to let them to stand up.

● How MTR can attract many passengers.

On the commuter departure time choice of any reference point researching hand, the departure time decisions of communters are of fundamental importance of peak period MTR traffic congestion. However, whether on the demand side, MTR underground train congestion relief measures, such as MTR ticket fare to every terminal station needs to be charged cheaper fare or discount fare in the peak (busy) time every day. To aim to attract many passengers to choose to catch MTR Underground train public transportation tools, substitute to choose other public transportation tools in the peak time.

Over the past decades, there have been very active research efforts in the departure time problem, both in econometric modeling and dynamic user equilibrium fields. Although, these works provide valuable insights into dynamic commuter decision making, they do not identify the commuters' response to gains and losses related to whole actual arrival time to reference points who may have relative. The appliability of the reference point hypothesis of prospect theory to the commuter's departure time decision making to obtain a better understanding of how departure time choice in MTR platform during their waiting underground train arrival time. However, every MTR underground train actual arrival time and deviation variables related to reference points (gains and losses) are the key factors in the departure time choice model. How the MTR underground train of every communter's daily departure time decision can be modelled when the reference point hypothesis of prospect theory. The MTR underground train's schedule delay is defined as the difference between the preferred arrival time (PAT) and the actual arrival time (AT) for a given MTR communter. In a daily MTR commute, a commuter in the indifference band actual arrival time is an essential feature of MTR schedule study. Two reference points are the earliest acceptable arrival time and the work starting time for a given MTR platform waiting passengers. In psychological view point, prospect theory proposes that the displeasure of a loss is perceived or greater than the pleasure of a gain of the same attitude and therefore, the value function is stronger for losses than gains.

To conclude, it seems that if MTR waiting passengers need not spend long time to wait underground train arrival in platform and it can provide seats to let them to sit down in the busy (peak) crowding time. It will make them to feel pleasure, even the MTR ticket fare is not fair and reasonable to charge higher fare to compare other kinds of public transportation tools fares. So the peak waiting time factor can influence the passengers to choose other kind of transportation tools to catch easily. Moreover, MTR's two reference points are the earliest role. Similarly a loss is observed when the MTR platform waiting commuter experiences or actual arrival time which is beyond that the MTR schedule time. Due to that a MTR waiting commuter is as an early side arrival of whose actual arrival time is earlier than whose preferred arrival time.

Q9 How and why shop facility management can influence consumer individual shopping behavior?

If it is possible, what shop facility management factors can influence their consumption decision when they enter the shop to plan to buy anything. I shall indicate some shop case studied to explain whether how and why every shop's facility management can influence consumer individual consumption desire when any one consumer enters any shops.

● Shop's low ceiling height location (FM) influence consumer behavior

Can the shop's ceiling height influence shoppers' shopping behavior? Can the shop's variation in ceiling height can influence how consumers process information to decide to make purchase decision in the shops, e.g. for this situation, when the consumer enters the shop, he/she feels the ceiling height is low and it has a lamp will contact his/her head in possible. So, he/she chooses to move far away from the low ceiling location in the shop. It is possible that shop's ceiling low height and the lamp locates at the ceiling low height position will influence many customers' choices to leave the low ceiling height and lamp location, then the shop's low ceiling height will have possible to influenced many customers to choose to find the another shop to buy the similar kind of products , due to the lamp locates in the low ceiling height, so this lamp and low ceiling height will be possible factor to influence any shoppers who won't choose to walk to this dangerous location in the shop. If the shop's all spaces are ceiling height and it has many lamps are located at the low ceiling height spaces. Then, it will be serious to cause many shoppers do not want to spend too much time to choose any products in the shop because they feel dangerous to walk to the any low ceiling height lamps' locations in the shop.

Hence, hoe to design the different concept may be activated by the showroom ceiling if it were relatively high, as it tends to be in mall stores, versus low, as it is in most strip mall shops and outlet centers. Relatively high ceilings may bring safe shopping emotion to let any consumers to feel thoughts related to freedom, whereas lower ceilings may let consumers to feel dangerous to walk the locations in any shops. Hence it seems any shops ought not neglect whether their ceiling height is tall and the lamps ought avoid to locate in any low ceiling height locations in order to influence consumers number to be decreased.

● Can house facility management influence consumer individual purchase intention?

When one new property is built, whether the property consumers will consider how the new property is facility to influence their purchase intention to the property will the new property's (FM) influence buyers in real estate markets' preferences choice and living interest. Any new property's internal characteristics of the house unit itself , such as rooms available, when example, of external are location, accessibility to utilities services and facilities will have possible to influence the property buyer's final property purchase decision, so it seems that even the property price is cheap, it is not represent the property buyer will choose to buy the property, if he/she feels the property's facility management is poorer to compare other similar kinds of properties.

So, it can help real estate analysts better explain and predict the behavior of decision makers in real estate markets. Property consumers will search for property information, concerns the property's quality, price distinctiveness, ability, facility management, service of the property's external environment to decide whether the property is high value to choose to buy to compare other kinds of properties.

However, the external environmental forces, such as limited resources, e.g. time or financial will influence whose property consumption choice and living the property's satisfaction feeling (represent) a feedback from post-property purchase reflection used to inform subsequent decisions. The process of the property buyer's leaving experience will serve to influence the extent to which the property consumer how to consider future next time property purchases decision and new information methods. Hence, when one property consumer chooses to buy a house, it refers house features are house internal attributes , such as quality of building, the design as well as internal and external design, which are important factors for a property consumer when he/she needs to select and purchases one house.

The other (FM) factors which can influence the property consumers' needs, include living space as features, such as the size of kitchen, bathroom, bedroom, living bath and other rooms available in the house. The environment of housing area is also important factor, e.g. the condition of the hood, attractiveness of the area, quality of houses, type of houses, type of houses, density of housing, wooded area or free coverage, slope of the attractive views, open space, non-residential uses in the areas vacant sites, traffic noise, level of owner-occupation in , level of education in level of income in, security from crime, quality of schools, religious of , transportation , shopping center, sport entertainment can be supplied to close to the house area. All these human related issue of the property's location will also influence the property buyer's living location selection. Hence, above (FM) influence property consumer purchase behavior, it is based on the relationship behavior. The consumer's house purchase intention and house features, living space, environment and distance to recreation center, supermarket, library etc. public facilities variable (FM) factors.

In conclusion, the house internal space facility management and external environment facility management factors will influence property consumer individual house purchase intention.

- The effects of in-store shelf design facility management factor influences consumer behavior

Can every store retailer's shelf design influence supermarket and large retail stores shoppers' behaviors when they visit the stores? However, currently many stores tend to build on traditional and repetitive design for their store shelf layout, it brings results in outdated store layouts.

Another important store shelf layout design aspect, retailer should consider carefully is the allocation of products on shelves. So, it seems that efficient shelf space allocation management does not only minimize the economic threats of empty product shelves, it can also lead to higher consumer satisfaction, a better customer relationship.

Why does supermarket shelves design is important? Any retail tore will sell product category within a shelf. They can use the same nominal category , e.g. crisps next to light crisps, same food product shelf. Anyway, a goal-based shelf display can contain several product, that determine a common consumer goal, e.g. fair trade. Hence, these two categorical product structuring methods are also described in terms of how to put product, or food on shelf benefit and attribute -based product categories.

These shelf design food or product storing method will have more influence consumers to choose to buy the supermarket or retail store food or products more easily , due to products, or food put on their shelf very convenient and systematic to attract consumers' shopping consideration to the supermarket or retail store.

- Music (FM) environment influence consumer consumption desire

Is it possible that shop music (FM) environment can raise consumer purchase desire? In one shop or supermarket, it can provide soft music (FM) equipment to let consumers can listen soft music or songs in the supermarket or retail shop when the are staying to spend more time shopping and whether soft music facility can be expected to raise customer individual value-added options to the music facility shop in the supermarket or retail shop.

Can the music facilities prolong consumers to stay in the store? It is possible that tempo soft music can influence consumers to stay longer time in restaurants and supermarkets and retail shops. It is possible that the different types of music (FM) in any supermarket, restaurant, retail shop owning music listening facility shopping environment. It will have possible to influence consumers to prolong staying in their shops. For example, one wine selling retail shop has classical music (FM) listening equipment to let consumers to listen when they enter the wine shop, it is possible to cause consumers to choose to buy more expensive wine products. Some researchers indicate when the wine shop owns classical music facility to let all consumers can list classical music when they walk in the wine ship, it can evoke the wine consumers to choose to buy purchasing higher prices wine products in the long term classical music listening environment. Otherwise, in a fitness sport center, musical fir and excite or popular music (FM) environment can attract fitness sport players' emotion to play and kind of fitness sport facility longer time. Also, in one supermarket, the soft music facilities listening environment can persuade or attract food consumers to spend more time in the mall consuming food or beverage also purchase other products more easily, due to they will listen soft music to be influenced to choose to prolong staying time in the supermarket. It seems that it has relationship between retail shop's music facility environment and consumer's emotion will be influenced by these different kinds of soft music or songs to raise consumption desire in the supermarket, if some consumers like to prolong to stay longer consuming time in the owning music facility environment's retail shop.

In fact, some researchers indicate the owning background music facility selling environment's ship , it can affect consumer decision making, memory, concentration consumption desire. So, classical , jazz soft music facility ought be installed in restaurants, retail shops, restaurants' environment. Otherwise, popular , exciting, noise, pop music facility ought be installed in fitness sport centers, theme park entertainment parks business places in order to influence fitness sport players or theme park entertainers to prolong playing or entertaining time to feel real sport or entertainment theme park playing machine facility's entertainment enjoyable feeling as well as attracting restaurant or supermarket or retail shop's consumers to prolong their staying time to make consumption decisions. Hence, it seems that music facility environment can raise consumers' consumption desire in possible.

- University bookstore atmospheric factors how to influence student's purchase book behavior?

Any university bookstore how to do international control and structuring of book internal environment to raise students' purchase book desires in university itself school's bookstore, it will be one popular question to any universities. Hence, whether the university bookstore internal (FM) factors include: lighting, music, colors, scents, temperature, layout and general cleanliness as well as university external factors include: the university bookstore shape/size, windows, university parking facility for students availability and location, which can play an influential role of the university bookstore image in order to influence the university itself students to choose to buy books from themselves bookstore or university outside bookstores.

Whether the university student needs to spend how long individual learning time and how much learning nervous to spend time to choose any kinds of book in the universiity bookstore or outside bookstores, this issue , he/she will consider. Because he/she does want to expect spend much time and nervous to choose to buy books in any bookstore. If the university's bookstore physical location and internal (FM) image can let its target student customers to feel it's all book products are stored in any attractive internal book shelves places, e.g. the cheapest and the most expensive different subjects of text books are stored in one system method to bring the positive image of value and quality in order to let university target student customers can find their books' choice location to spend less time to search any books to read in the unviersiity bookstore easily.

However, due to learning time is shortage to every university student of the university's book shelves can display all text books in the attractive right locations in the university bookstore as well as the university's bookstore ought has an adequate space to let university students to walk to anywhere and find any subjects of text books and compare their book sale prices in the bookstore's any shelves' locations easily when they walk to the subject of book shelf location, then they can make accurate decision either to buy the right kind of subject book or not buy it to read in the short time. They will feel their book choice purchase decision making process won't influence their learning time in themselves universiity. Then, the university students will be influenced by themselves university's bookstore's attractive external university facilities in the university's any teaching places and the university's bookstore internal attractive environment facility image which can influence the students to make final choices to buy their liking books to read from their university's itself bookstore. Hence, the university's bookstore internal and external building environment (FM) design factors will influence its students whether choose to buy from themselves bookstore or another outside general bookstore.

● How and why does retail atmospheric environment influence consumers behavior in retail shop?

Any shop's internal facility management design can influence atmospheric environment to influence consumer individual shopping desire, e.g. colour, lighting, music, crowding, design and layout factors, which internal shop (FM) environment can influence the first time shopping visiting client ' cognitive process how to feel the shop store image. Such as if the store's (FM) environment can bring enjoyable and fun and happy image to let them to feel shopping's enjoyment.

In conclusion, when consumers will like to stay longer time in the store. Due to the store's internal (FM) atmospheric environment can attract them to stay longer time in the store. Then, the customer's shopping value will raise and it can bring purchasing intention and shopping satisfaction. How can (FM) influence retail atmospheric physical (FM) environment ? Can (FM) bring indirect relationship to influence how the consumer individual causes positive or negative purchase intention when he/she has influence to prolong staying desire in the store, when the shop has good (FM) , it will bring long time to make consumption chance in the shop.

Q10 Can facility management (FM) quality influence consumer satisfactory service feeling?

Any organization's facility management can improve the effectiveness of the maintenance organization. It can provide improved operational and maintenance functions to maintain the physical environment to support the overall mission. However, any organization will consider whether it improves its facilities, it will raise consumer satisfactory feeling when it provides the service to them, e.g. education service industry, when students need to often to attend any school's classrooms or lecture halls, computer rooms, libraries, all these facilities will be student's learning environment. If these school facilities can be maintenance to let students to feel comfortable to enjoy to study in their schools' any learning locations. Then, it has possible that to bring their enjoyable learning feeling in theirs schools.

● How school's facility management influences student's learning satisfactory feeling.

However, in education industry case, the school's facility management has those criteria can be used to measure effectiveness. Student individual response time between the student's request for computer use service in school computer rooms, library reading service in school library , classroom computer facilities and tables, chairs etc. furniture supplies service and the facility management supply number and available to useful time. If the student believes that the response time is too long when he/she feels need to use any school facilities, the actual number of seconds or minutes, he/she needs to wait how long time to queue to use his/her school's any facilities in library, classroom, computer room. So, the student's queue waiting time to use any his/her school's facilities, it can measure the school's facility management effectiveness.

● Scheduling of preventive maintenance activities.

It schedules of any maintenance activities are not arranged effectively to the school. Then, it will influence students' poor learning facility service to their school. For their situation, when the school's first floor has two men toilets are damaged. They are needed to be required. However, it is one week period, the first floor 100 students can not use the first floor men toilets. Hence, in this week, all 100 students need to go to other floors toilets to often use. They will feel busy and time is not enough when they need to attend to any classrooms to listen the first floor classrooms teachers' lesson. If he/she arrives the first floor classroom too late, due to he/she needs to go to another floor male toilets to queue to use. Then, he/she will feel angry and worries about whose absent or late attending classroom behavior when the lesson's teacher has attended early in the first floor classroom , and he teacher will need him/her to explain why he/she will go to this classroom lately, if his/her explanation won't be accepted to attend to the first floor classroom too late in the week. So, arrangement maintenance schedule to any school's facilities issue is importnt to influence student's satisfactory feeling to the school. Also, lacking of preventive maintenance activities will bring results in unscheduled shutdown of critical equipment can have an unrecoverable impact on the school's good learning environment providing to student's mission.

In fact, however in any organizations, such as school, ship, office etc. organizations, achieving balance of effectiveness and efficient difficulties and takes time and effort on the part of management and staff. It is not enough to establish an optimal relationship between these two parts. It has another factor that organizations need to consider costs. In today's budget tightening environment, decreasing expenses requires accepting a lower level of efficiency and effectiveness. The goal is to determine the point at which decreasing efficiency and effectiveness is no longer acceptable before that point is reached.

It brings this question : How to apply facility management knowledge to rise efficiency and effectiveness in order to improve quality standard of service to satisfy consumers' needs in short time? Such as school's facilities service case. What factors can influence student's level of satisfaction with regards to higher educational facilities services? It seems that any school's facilities will influence its students how to satisfy its education service indirectly. Because they need often to go to school to learn. So, any school's facilities, e.g. classrooms, computer rooms, libraries, toilets, lecture halls, canteens, sport and entertainment centers, research laboratories, school car parks, student enquiry counters, all these places to the school's any students will attend. So, how raise schools' facilities improvement to satisfy students' learning needs in the school's any locations which will have help to influence it student individual satisfaction level to the school's service, instead of every teacher individual teaching performance service to the school's students.

For any service organizations , such as hotels, restaurant, financial institutions, retail stores and hospitals etc. The physical environment can influence how customers' evaluation of their service. Due to service has intangible nature, so customers will rely on evaluate service quality.

Any higher education institutions are education service providing organizations. They need have comfortable and enjoyable educational environment to be provided to the students to attend the school's any places in order to meet whose learning expectations and studying experience needs. So, the school's facility management will be one factor to influence student's learning satisfaction when they expect to attend the school's any locations or places to let them to feel the school's learning environment have good facility management feeling.

In fact, if the school has comfortable classrooms or lecture halls educational environment to let its students to feel, it will bring assistance to raise their learning satisfactory feeling. So, comfortable learning facility management environment is one kind of school's facility service characteristics, it includes intangibility, perishability, inseparability and variability. So, they are every student individual learning feeling when they are attending to the school's any learning locations. So, school's facility management service feeling will influence whether they expect to choose this school to study. If the school's facility management learning environment is more comfortable and teaching facilities are better to compare other schools' facilities. Then, it will have possible to attract many students to choose this school to study. Such as any educational organizations, instead of the teachers (lecturers and professors) whose educational level is influence students number. The university's building environment will influence students' learning feeling, when they attend in the university. The facilities include laboratories, lecture theatres an offices, but also residential accommodations, catering facilities, sports and recreations centers because university students need have university life feeling to let them to fell the university can give welfare services , e.g. medical services, career guidance, sport entertainment, residential accommodation etc. service, instead of educational learning service in classrooms and lecture theatres. Hence, university's diversification facilities services are needed to satisfy university students to choose it to study, instead of university teacher's educational performance.

When one student can enroll the university to study from secondary education institution. The admitted student will usually consider two aspects to decide to choose the university to study. One aspect is the academic programs, of sequence of courses choices and the another aspect is the university's facilities whether they can satisfy their university life need, e.g. library, dorms, bookstore, food canteen , gym's sport entertainment, education technological facilities in the classrooms and lecture theatres to let the students to feel the university's teaching facilities are achieved his/her learning demand.

So, these two factors (teaching and learning and facilities) are linked to each other to influence student's total school learning experience and attitude towards a particular institution and this is termed as value chain in the student's learning process in the university. Hence, student individual evaluation variables will include teaching staff, teaching method, enrolment and facility enough supply actual service need.

However, the university's facilities, such as any residential accommodation, canteen, library , classroom, lecture theatre, sport gym, entertainment center will be their useful facilities need to satisfy their learning, entertainment and eating ,even living need in residential accommodation in the school's learning life experience every day. If one student chooses to live in the university residential accommodation . All of his/her learning and eating and living time and spending will be calculated to the university's any facilities to let him/her to feel it can provide enough facilities to let him/her to enjoy.

Hence, the facility management factor, such as overall campus environment, library, laboratory, classroom, lecturer theatre size and facility supply of on campus accommodation, welfare right service, parking areas, cafeteria , sport center etc. They will be every students facilities service needs from the university supplies choice. So, any university ought not neglect how to improve itself university's space area facilities to achieve satisfy their needs after they choose this university to study. Hence, any university's facility management will influence how the student's satisfactory learning service feeling when he/she chooses the university to study.

In conclusion, better facility management will attract more students to choose the university to study. Otherwise, worse facility management will not attract more students to choose to study the school. Hence, it seems that the school's facility management factor has relationship to influence student's satisfactory feeling, instead of teacher individual teaching performance factor to the school.

Q11 Can hotel facilities influence hotel consumer choice ?

Travellers choose hotel to live. They will consider price, room comfortable feeling, hotel location , gum sport or entertainment service facility supplies , hotel room booking service etc. factors to decide whether the hotel can achieve every traveller individual minimum living need. However, whether hotel facilities factor will be the main factor to influence travellers' living needs. How and why do travellers consider hotel facilities whether are enough supply or facilities of quality to satisfy their demand to cause their living choice to the hotel final decision.

Usually, hotel's customers won't plan to live too long time, e.g. more than three months in the hotel. Because they are travelling aim. It will bring this question: Does hotel facilities quality consider to influence their hotel living choice if the traveller is short-term traveller to the country? However , some travellers who have effort to spend money to live high class hotels, even their journey is short trip. Hence it seems that short trip , hotel living reason can not influence the high class hotel travellers' living comfortable demand to the high class hotel room. Hence , the high class hotel room's facility management quality is also needed high performance. Even, when they need to eat breakfast, lunch , dinner in the high class hotel canteens or playing any sport equipment, or gum equipment or wathching movie in the hotel's small cinema room . They must need high class hotel can supply more entertainment, restaurant , sport facilities to satisfy their comfortable needs in the high class hotel. Moreover, they must consider safety issue when they are living in the high class hotel. So, thy must demand the hotel have enough five fright equipment in their rooms, or corridors and the stairs to let them can leave the dangerous locations to arrive the most safe locations immediately when the hotel has fire accident occurrence in any where . So, it ensures that the high class hotel's customers must ensure the high class hotel's facilities can satisfy their any one of above these needs before they decide to live this high class hotel.

In fact, high class hotel's room price must be more expensive to compare the low class hotel. So, it explains why high class hotel's consumers will need the hotel has safe and good quality of facilities to let them to feel it is one reasonable price, safe , good service and good facilities' high class hotel to live. Usually, when the traveller arrives the country to travel, the travelers chooses the hotel to live, it is whose first time visit in common. So, he/she ought consider that the hotel environment seems it is good or bad to let the traveller to select to live. If the hotel's facility environment is new and beauty and design colorful to let the first time travellers to feel. Then, it is possible that good facilities environment can influence the first time travellers to select to live, even the hotel's room price is more expensive to compare other similar hotels in the travelling living places. Hence, it explains why hotel facilities can influence traveller individual room booking choice. When he/she is the first time to visit the hotel to select whether to live or not.

CHAPTER THREE

Marketing theory

Q1 What are the differences between multi level marketing and direct personal sale?

It seems that multi level marketing (MLM), netwrok marketing and direct sellers scheme marketing which are under the pyramid retail sales criterion. It means only third parties with no connection to the selling organizations are considered legitimate "ultimate users". Consequently, it deems the consumption of product by distributors (participants), "internal consumption" to be illegalitimate and simply a cover for fraud.

As multi level marketing or direct sellers from pyramid schemes both marketing which need individual participant or distributor who give money to buy their products to join to whose business to earn commissions. It seems the participant or distributor will be client role more than member or business partnership role. So, it seems MLM or direct sellers from pyramid schemes which main income sources are come from participants or distributors (internal clients). Rather, the key question is to determine whether the purchasers, whoever who may be actually resell or consume their products if the sales transactions are thus reveals to legitimate, as a matter of economic principle. They are also revealised to have increased social welfare. By accepting and adopting without further inquiry the "retail sales criterion", even though it is contrary to basic principles of economics and logic. Consequently, I shall indicate these above proposed test to distinguish legitimate from fraudulent enterprise of legitimacy to multi level marketing or pyramid schemes direct sellers both sale channels.

The reasons of legitimacy to multi level marketing or pyramid schemes direct sellers include which are inappropriately not just the consumer surplus flowing from, but also the profits that the parent firm earns from selling products to dustributors for their internal consumption. This error is caused by asserting that the resulting biased estimates of cash flow are sufficient to indicate that either a pyramid scheme (multi level or direct personal sale) is in progress. These both network sale channels discard all profits earned with internal consumption and because they assume, without the justificaton or validation, that all participants (distributors) in a direct selling enterprise act to as to maximize their cash income. What is the mean of relating high rate at which individuals are to direct selling is sufficient to be defrauded. It is alternative explanations for the rate at which individuals quit direct selling (the "quit rate"), and it provides no economic analysis or inquiry as to the quit rate those distributors might exhibit outside direct selling. It implies the quit rate of distributors in either direct selling or multi level (network) enterprise is pyramid scheme comparable to what one might observe in the counter-factual in which those individuals are employed as wage labour.

As the accounting theory view, pyramid multi level marketing fraud is considered of circumstances unrelated to pyramid fraud, such as calculations of distributors (participants) income whether a parent company's current cash outflows are fully funded by inflows. More direct personal sale or phyramid theme sale business calculations in this regard are biased toward finding fraud because which discard all profits earned with internal consumption and because which assume without theoretical justification or validation that all participants in a direct selling enterprise act as to maximize their cash income. Alternative explanation for the rate at which individuals quite direct selling the quit-rate and provides no economic analysis might exhibit outside direct selling. In fact, a high rate is sufficient to conclude that distributors (participants) were defrauded is apparent upon noting that there are also high quit-rates in other undeniably legitimate businesses. A direct selling (pyramid) of only a few distributors are able to build businesses that six and seven figure annual incomes is similiarly. Chief Executive officer and the distribution of salaries at many commercial entities exhibits a pyramidal form that logic would conclude that all corporations must be considered pyramid fraudsters in the labour market. Even of an economic analysis is well intentioned from direct personal sale market or pyramid enterprises in any countries. The politicies of different countries governments advocated and other misinterpretations, impose costs on consumers, producers and society at large. An objective appraisal of the costs and benefits with using test that are generated false positives represents the first step toward a meaning ful; analysis of the appropriate public policy.

This direct personal sale or pyramid direct sales scheme is concluded by providing an examination of the costs and benefits of regulation and increased enforcement. It seems direct personal sale market has no any legal doctrine support that only sales to third parties constitute legitimate business activity and application of logic and the misinterpretation and misapprehension of prior court rulings that have biased inquiries into the potential to generate false positives. So, some economists have failures of logic and economic that have characterized prior evaluations of public policy low and pyramid schemes or direct sale market.

Our goal is to providing some guiding principles to indicate economically sensible, how a true pyramid scheme or direct personal sale market can be identified and the costs and benefits of different approaches as to how fraud should be detected, with MLM and pyramid direct sale schemes. Otherwise, Multi level market, MLM compensates not only in the form of commissions on sales to distributors (participants), but it also compensate commissions on the sales of it's recurits. The fact, that the share prices of MLM enterprises that have one public have remained positive indicates that the market believes MLM enterprises have value and that this value will be sustained. In constrast, a direct personal sale market enterprise is unsustainable, e.g. a pyramid scheme that will collapse. Or always faces the threat of being shut down as a fraud by regulators, would not be able to sustain positive market value. It is important to note that legitimate multi level network direct selling benefits not just the parent firm and distributors, but also businesses and society at large. A MLM's products may require its salespeople to invest meaningful time and effort in educating the client as to the benefits of the product, resulting in a long sales cycle before sale is concluded. MLM provides the opportunity to every participant (distributor) to build to personal networks to introduce potential purchases to products. As a matter of economic principle of revealed preference or revealed profitability. Similarly, consumers who choose to purchase from legitimate MLM network direct sellers, they perceive more value in purchasing from a direct seller relative to other alternatives.

Many distributors join the MLM to purchase a preferred product at a lower price. Other distributors find MLM is a convenient way of support their income on their terms and according to their needs, for example by working why reasonally or part time. Another participants may find that participation in a entry point into a center or business opportunity to invest in their human capital and to acquire a network of business connections. Other participants may find that MLM (network selling) is the perfect match for their talents and skill sets. The goodwill to MLM is needed to concern. Consequently, consumer protection efforts have focused on identifying. Because, same MLM enterprises pretend to be legitimate direct sellers, such as fraudsters' debase the goodwill are trust that legitimate direct selling has established with consumers. Resultly, the direct personal sale enterprises pretend to do legitimate business activities to influence the unhealth or poor economic growth in societies. Otherwise, the Multi level market (MLM) or network market enterprises can do more legitimate business activities to influence the health or poor economic growth in societies.

However, muli level marketing , MLM is as a very popular business model in the Western countries. It is a kind of the method of distribution of products. The method of building a sales network, it is one of the safest carries a very low risks ways of conducting business activity. The enter is to any markets, it is usually with market entry barriers and huge capital needs. Lack of expansion and lack of awareness of common practices. In the traditional business model, the risk of failure is very high. Also, unknown is the uncertain concerning the return on investments. However, despite high level of risk, this is the most popular business model.

So, multi level marketing is also called "network marketing". It is one of the fastest developing and still the least understand methods if introducing products to the market. It is mainly due to poor understanding of the system that multi level marketing is often regarded as network sales, pyramid sales or even pyramid schemes. It is marketing strategy and way of functioning of a company and its partners' independent distributors. Multi level marketing is a branch of direct sale. It involves offering products and services directly to clients on the basis of individual contacts, usually at direct's home, workplace or in other locations outside permanent retail sale branches. It is a form of sale outside, a traditional ship chain. It allows sellers to build personal structures of partners, who provide additional commissions from their sales. Every seller in multi level marketing has an opportunity to build own structure of salesman in which everyone is rewarded based on the marketing plan valid for each company. At the same time, achieving higher earnings, it is as a marketing strategy, way of functioning of a company and a system allowing to build individual network for independent distributors, classifying it has a branch of direct sales is a big mistake.

What is it's differences to pyramid scheme, MLM or network market and direct personal sale method? First, MLM is a retail sale, which is the most basic form of distribution carried out by means of a retail branch, e.g. grocery shop, chemist's shop department store, online auction site. Second, direct personal sale method is covering ususally the sale of insurance, kitchen wave houses etc. products. In this model of distribution commission from sold products goes only to the seller, who can't build network of his distributors. In order to sell products or services offered by a particular company, who has to be employed in the company as a sales representative. This means that who works for the owner of a company, the company's whose employer, thus the sales representative doesn't work for whose own benefit as in case of personal direct sale marketing. Third, direct personal sale marketing is transferring a product or service from the producer of service provider to the consumer. Otherwise, MLM, Multi level marketing is as a system of rewarding people who contribute to sale of products or provision of services. In the multi level marketing method people contributing to sale are those who recommend a purchase directly from a particular company. The employee whose is provided in course of making an order is rewarded for a recommendation resulting in actual sale, as the bonus system is usually multi level and allows generating passive income, income is not the direct effect of the work of recommending person. This works, this way is as every person has the opportunity to build individual consumer distribution structurer. In order words, multi level system rewards for directly recommended persons and recommended directly by direct ones. Fourth, MLM, it means mail order sale, this kind of distribution is characterized by lack of retail points in which products could be exchanged for money. The client makes an order directly in the company after learning about its offer on television, in telephone conversation or from a received catalogue. Finally, direct personal sale method is an illegal organization of sales, which is often mistaken for muti level marketing. One of the main reasons for an illegal organization is presented as a multi level system. The difference that makes pyramids illegal and multi level making legal is the inability to distribute a product or provide service. If there are no sales of a product, it is impossible to take about marketing companies by promising high sales convince participants to pay high one off about of money that allows then to participate in the programme which makes it impossible for participants to generate sales, as all payments go to the account of those organizing the business. Thus, direct personal sale is nothing like multi level marketing or network marketing . MLM, in which sale is always based on a product or service and the commission system rewards participants depending on the contribution, regardless of held position. So, MLM, it is a network created based on contacts and ties between people and the participation of all members of the network in this activity.

Q2 Can multi level lmarketing can assist organizational development ?

We can view multi level marketing from two perspectives, one of them is the point of view of concept, the producer or the company for which multi level marketing is one of possible ways of introducing a new product to the market bearing huge cost with promotion and without the need to transfer rights to a product to someone. The second perspective is the point of view of an independent distribution for whom multi level marketing is a model of business which doesn't require a concept or bearing the risk with investing capital, as in case of typical business activity or franchising, such an approach makes it possible to define MLM as method of distribution of products, in which costs associated with advertising and marketing are covered at the moment of actual sale. Sales are fueled by clients of the MLM company who use their contacts to recommend the purchase of particular products. The

MLM company rewards the recommending person with a commission calculated based on the company's marketing plan for a recommendation ending with actual sale. Any marketing plan creates the possibility to generate unlimited revenues and at the same time eliminate risk with the necessity to invest substantial capital required to launch typical business activity.

How Multi level marketing can assist socio-economic development. For example, insurance business is a kind of MLM business, whether it can assist socio-economic development for long term. In insurance sector, insurance companies are looking for innovative methods to spread the message and maximum business in the short time. Many local MLM companies having quite large spread in the market with leading insurance brands to promote their insurance products along with their own products. Insurance sector makes available long time debt for the economic development of the country. At the same time, the MLM route provides employment opportunities and enhances their social status. The MLM members have opportunity to develop themselves personally. This multipe rise of MLM companies can be looked at as a social contribution and these insurance MLM companies or cooperatives are as a development oriented social movement. How insurance sector can assist the economic and social impact of MLM as a tool which can influence society through employment generation, mobilzing long term funds and improving quality of life of people. There has opportunity to attractive propective candidates to gain network marketing companies. Past studies indicated the fact that a 100 % annual turnover rate among sales personnel in certain network marketing company is not unusual. According to the Direct Selling Association in th United States, it indicated 70% of the revenue from the direct selling industry was generated by network marketing companies and most of this come from the better known companies, such as Amway, was multi level instead of single level compensation plans. Such as India, network marketing was in India during mid 90 year was followed by the establishment of the Indian arm of Amway corporation The total turnover of network marketing companies in India was estimated at $30,104 rising in 2005 year with an annual growth rate of 25%.

It seems Amway can assist USA Government to earn much taxation income and sale income to reduce USA unemployment rate. As, Amway exports to India market. Indian Direct Selling Association (IDSA) facilitates membership to build network marketing companies. So, India is a good network marketing for Amway MLM company. However, consumers often have negative perceptions of direct selling organizations and network marketing organization in particular. The aggressive selling techniques, exaggeration of facts in network marketing organization recruiting and pyramiding scams together toward a basis for this negative perception. Network marketing is a subset of direct selling and is also known as multi level marketing structure marketing or multi level direct selling. Network marketing can best be described as a direct selling channel that focuses heavily on its compensation plan because the distributors (members of the networks) may receive compensation in two fundamental ways. First, sales people (distributors) may earn compensation from their personal sales of products and services to the consumers (non-member of the network). Second, they may earn compensation from sales to purchase from those persons whom who have personally sponsored or recruited into the network (down lines), these down lines continue sponsoring or recruiting to the network sharing the benefits with their sponsors or recruiters (up lines). So, the aim of MLM network market which reward sales agents for buying products and selling products and finding other agents to buy and sell products. In common, the agents (distributors) or participants can earn marketings ranges from 20% to 50% of sales income. In addition, distributors can also receive a monthly commission for their personal volume which is the value of every product who personally buy or sell. Further, the distributors also receive a net commission on the sales of those who recruit into the networks. It seems that the sales developed network marketing are not developed from sales created by retailing, but also developed through recruiting or sponsoring independent distributors. Thus, as distributors continue to recruit or sponsor not distributors to expand whose network, the new distributors will contribute new sales to the network and gain commission in return. This hunge incentive makes the investment in insurance very attractive for a member. For example, coverage margin on first premium for insurance policies can earn the range of 30% to 40%. This given the leverage for structuring the insurance sale through MLM. MLM is a marketing function in which sales people are paid for their personal contribution as well as for the persons who recruit in to the function or process. Employees or sales people who are individual team to work from which who get a reward on the achievement sale force. So, who can sense much ideas to help marketing organizations to raise high demand when demand is too high and the current employees can't meet those are recruits come in the till the position. So, employees are encouraged to bring many employees to the organization.

MLM is also a very important function in providing jobs for the jobless. The recruitment process looks for young jobless people and earns them on income from which who can support themselves. It is happy feeling to know that you are working and at the same time providing opportunities for the loss fortunate to support them. You have chance to increase your paid if you introduce someone to work as participant or recruit or distributer role to any MLM market. It will reduce the numbers of unemployment of the insurance company in society. The idea presents people with great and better learning of the MLM strategy. When people are recruited in to the business, who are trained about its functions. This training acts as a good way of future advancements in the field. It also helps those individuals to use the knowledge to their advantage once who leave to job to enter marketing or sale career.

The job presents flexibility in hours work. Due people can work at any time who feel fits in them schedule. It can also train them to learn how to achieve whose sale target and attempt to do own business and no and captial spending. Is network marketing or multi level selling marketing as it is called all about getting rich quick with minimal effort? Multi level marketing or network marketing means referring products or services directly to consumers within your network. It involves building a network. For each referral is made by the network. The preceding link or upline as those individuals are called in network marketing terms, gets a certain percentage of commission. MLM, network marketing doesn't need you to be a user of the product or service that you would eventally be referring within your network. Network marketing or MLM only need you put ability to put in lots of hard work. In fact, twice as much as in a regular job or business, willingness to learn new diversified skills, ability to discipline your ability to be as network with like minded people who can help you. So, MLM can help unemployment people to find either freelance or temporary or permanent kinds of position choices, such as sales person or distributor role in MLM company.

So, network (MLM) marketing can offer various benefits to them like, lower initial costs of setting your business excellent training and product/service knowledge from industry experts, opportunity to earn additional residual income with a greater chance to move into a full time earned income model, flexibility to work at your own pace and time choice of retiring whenever you want.

Network market can be kind of multi level marketing. As network marketing is confronted with a number of issues that include the continuous erosion of campaign effectiveness, the fragmentation of traditional markets, the disappearance of the vendors' information advantage and significant changes in the distribution channel. Based on established building blocks of marketing and social network theory, a conceptual framework called network theory to integrate the two fields in a systematic way.

The networked marketing framework provides a structure for identifying the customer social network's impact on the marketing effectiveness in the different customer lifecycle phases and suggests the use of certain tools to acqire knowledge about the nature and the functional details of the social influence. However, the network marketing framework was tested in a setting on an international sample of a large company's customer database. How customer social network activity with an impact on marketing is the most intense in the purchase phase and the least. Hence, in the awareness phase, as well as the fact, that product and communication are the mix areas most impacted by social networks. For example, health care is an individual necessity and kind of national luxury product of a kind of multi level decision models. Due to health care is neither a necessity or a luxury, it is both since the income elasticity varies with the level of analysis. With insurance, individual income elasticities are typically near zero, when national health expenditure elasticities and commonly greater. It is to expected that measured income elasticities will differ for an individual, a risk-pooling group, or a national health system, just as price elasticities for individual, firm and market demand normally differ from each other. In past, some economists indicate income elasticity of individual, health expenditures under insurance (usually 60% to 95% of total spending) is typically near zero or negative, when the elasticity of national health expenditures with respect to national income is typically greater than 1.0. So, it seems individual income level and health factor has close relationship to decide to buy any health insurance policies.

Whether how multi level decision model quickly resolves to make evident the role of social and private insurance in linking micro and macro analysis in health economics. Within an insurance group, the bulk of the health resources will be allocated to those individuals who are ill and to get benefits from medical care. Individual budget constraints and ability to play concerns are pooled insurance financing. The contrast between the behaviour of the average individual, and the behaviour of the group to buy medical health insurance mean is well illustrated by insurance. However, medical health insurance pools are not only likely to display separation between group and individual behaviour, who are designed to bring about such a separation. The purpose of medical health insurance is to remove the individual budget constraint, and to reduce or eliminate the influence of cost of care on patient's and physician's decisions of how much care to use. If persons are fully insured, correlations with measures of individual income provide no information about income effects per each, e.g. the effect of monetary budget constraints, but instead reflect the influence of other unmeasured variables, cost of time, family resources, education, preferences etc. that are correlated with an individual's income. Hence, it seems that multi level model of determinants of pyramid or network sale method is suitable to sell in health insurance market. In any country's health insurance market, it will have two kind groups of people who will feel who have need to buy health medical insurance product. One group is without purchase any health medical insurance product , and another group owns health medical insurance product . At the macro level, income effects are still strong to influence anyone to decide to buy health medical insurance product, but variation factor due to differences in health status can also influence anyone to decide to buy health medical insurance product . With the country's people who feel need of health medical product, the pooling of funds will remove the insurance market income constraints and tends to strengthen the correlation of individual health status with expenditures. However, individual income effects still dominate the insurance market in the health medical insurance any country. So, it seems that health medical product insurance will have large share to lead to any country's insurance product income among of the travel insurance, accident insurance, life insurance, car insurance, employee welfare insurance etc. different kinds of insurance products market in any country. So, mulit level marketing shall be suitable to enter insurance product sale market.

Direct sale represents a modern product distribution system directly to consumer. Generally, directly to their homes, to their workplace or other places, besides retail shops. Ths best known type of direct sale, the network marketing or multi level marketing implies the existence of a network of distributors which earn income from selling on commission, to which who add the trade marketing. So, insurance, travel agent, share broker, property agent etc. these occupations which can belong to multi level or network marketing.

Following, I shall discuss the another kind of multi level marketing, e.g. franchise business. Franchise means the field of activity in which it was used. It is a license allowing the designee to sell and market a company's products or services in a particular place, using the name or the trade mark of the company, e.g. Mc Donald fast food restaurant. It allows whom to do business for the franchise owner, but not through the franchise owner. From the marketing point of view, franchise represents a distribution system based on the partnership between two parties which are legally independent. Between the franchisor (the proprietary owner, the owner of the trade mark of products and services) and the franchisee. However, developing a franchise using a well known trade mark, so it is a more complex distribution system in multi level marketing view point. Also, franchise business can be sold from internet sale channel in the multi level marketing technological view point.

Why the internet has positive influence on direct sale industry in multi level market to assist economic growth.

However, an important factor for increasing the turnover generated by direct sale companies and multi level marketing network represents a structure that is continuously changing. As technological changing, internet invention can raise the MLM sale method of chance. In multi level sale marketing, as house agent or franchise sale agent, insurance agent, share agent etc. these kind of occupations who can expand their businesses market from internet. Some of the trends indicate strong growth multi level products in international market. Also, high participation of women in multi level marketing, women are begining to realize that the internet makes it possible for them to reinvent themselves and begin a multi level business that requires little risk and low start up cost, such as internet sale method, these are no age limit to develop the multi level internet sale channel business and internet sale business can be an important market shares for household products in multi level marketing globally.

Besides these trends, the internet has positive influence on direct sales industry. Internet has had an impact in relations between direct seller and the company and between the direct seller and the consumer. The main multi levels through which the internet helps the development of multi level sale industry. Due to the internet has allowed direct sellers and customers to maintain contact outside the face to face meetings, it also allows direct sellers can use blogs and social media page to sell whose products, direct sellers can use electronic mailings and have online access to products and services brochures, the customers can pay to buy any online products through internet banking conveniently, more and more people were extended his professional activities of direct selling through the use of the internet and social networks, a direct selling activity can be run from home and doesn't require a high investment. Some may even give follow up orders by electronic means.

From the seller's point of view, the major attraction of direct selling is that internet sale channel offers an equal and flexible income opportunity to men and women, across all ages, level of experience and social origins. In the multi level marketing view point, the direct selling industry development trends will be direct influence by maintaining these advantages for the distributors and by using and developing the communicating modern technologies. So internet sale channel will be the potential multi level marketing to influence how to distribute products or service and to through direct sales and mulit level marketing are determined by a set of economic technological and even social factors.

Q3 Can multi level marketing can influence economic growth in poverty countries?

I feel that the role of multi level marketing in poverty countries to influence economic growth is important. For example, some businesses who need to manufacture and sell whose products to clients directly. So who need to set up factories and to open shops in local and overseas markets. It seems who need to exploit and save many investors loading more minimal amounts to prepare to sell immediately. It will raise recruiting new downlines and high cost of products as well as who also need to establish production plants in themselves countries or foreign countries to exploit local or overseas economics and to reduce the numbers of unemployment, among many other benefits. It seems the role of multi level marketing can reduce poverty countries unemployment ratio from internet sale channel, e.g. online salesperson , delivered products service and website design technician or computer technician etc. different website related positions will be created to sell to any online buyers conveniently from online sale channel.

Multi level marketing, e.g. online sale channel method can assist any country's businessmen to sell whose products to overseas easily. So, multi level marketing is one global sale market. Such online businesses that empower the people by providing opportunities to the first time businessmen to start businesses to sell their products to overseas market from internet (online sale) channel easily in the beginning. Moreover, multi level marketing has the potential of being a good source for job creation, income generation to sell products to any countries' buyers from online sale channel by websites contact conveniently at their homes.

Whether multi level marketing can solve poverty challenge. If multi level marketing deliberately target the poor as recruits, what role does multi level marketing play in income generation? Is there any relationship between MLM and job creation? Does multi level marketing (MLM) lead to skill and personal development of MM distributors? There are several appraches to poverty challenges. Examining them provides a necessary understanding of the nature of poverty. There are five main approaches to cause poverty challenge: The economic growth, the basic needs of rural development, the target and employment creation approaches. First, the economic growth approach would be leaded to distribution of income by the participation of the poor. In fact, economic growth need long time to develop in any countries. Also, multi level marketing, e.g. online sale channel needs a long time to build online buyer numbers to sell to different countries from distributors' websites globally. It seems this online sale method can assist global economic growth to give benefits to the developing countries to poverty people to solve unemployment challenges during any online businessmen build their websites to sell any products for long term. So, solving poverty challenge is needs long term time to develop any country's economy growth. Multi level marketing can be one of online sale method to solve unemployment challenge to poverty countries globally. Second, the rural development approach recognizes that poverty is multi dimensional. Thus, it aims at providing basic necessities of life, such as food, clean water, shelter, education, health care, and employment to rural dwellers in general. However, the limitation of this approach is that it doesn't directly target the poor. Again, decisions on rural areas to target may be done from political motives. Third, Target approach specifically aims at certain groups in the implementation of poverty programs, e.g. provision of social safety nets, micro credit and school meal programmes etc. Finally, employment creation approach emphasises the need to eliminate unemployment and underemployment. This will be achieved by creating employment from online sale channel.

The whole concept of multi level marketing is relatively new to any European and Western countries where which have existed for long term. For example, the DVD disc is a conglometrate of all firms that distribute to buyer contact in location away from fixed areas, like retail stores particularly at home. It is the locational characteristic that distinguishes it from other forms of personal selling. Multi level marketing is a subset of the DVD disc distributors are used in selling company products and also in recruiting other distributors. As a result, they receive compensation for their sales and from sales of those individuals who recruit. The senior distributors are called uplines when their recruits are called downlines. Other common products sold through multi level marketing include health and fitness product, cosmetics, cleaning agents, electrical appliances and several others which are popular to sell from this MLM marketing either network market or/and online market both methods.

It is very important to influence many multi level marketing companies do not incur any cost on advertisement since who can use internet to advertise whose products in their websites to let global online buyers to discover after they type the seller's website address to enter their websites at home conveniently. The distributors in MLM are usually organized into networks structure connection. Two main types of such structures are the binary and unilevel structure. The former allows just two direct downlines at each level and the other direct recruits are to be placed at different levels in the network of downlines. On the other hand, the unilevel structure permits the recruitment of an unlimited number of downlines. Direct selling firms usually opt between two choices either employees or independent distributors. There are no salaries or other fixed costs associated with recruitment of independent distributors. So a non selective recruitment used with a straight method of compensation often tends to draw poverty people easily earned incomes from only a modest commitment in time and effort. It seems to commission income method. The recruitment of a new distributor allows for only a single connection. However, double registration of a single distribution is not compatible with the MLM compensation plan. A distributor is allowed to participate in three activites of the MLM company's purchase of the products as users, sale to customers and access to mark up profit and recuritment that expansion of the network occurs. The diffusion of the product or service in the market is stimulated strong by the consumption or purchase of the product.

The benefits to MLM offers to distributors include low start cost, distributors can enjoy from the income of others, e.g. the downlines benefit in the distribution network of online sale to different advertisers can help the distributor to advertise whose products to earn commission income from website; online retail group volume and other bonuses and incentives, personal development via training and business support materials to sell from online sale channel, enhanced enterpreneurial spirit to sell products from onlibe channel globally, improved interpersonal skills and increased self confidence and jobs creation from online sale channel.

Nowadays, estimate that 97% of products are purchased and use consumption, which are consistent with legitimate multi level marketing to earn commission income, e.g. a online sale channel is more than a pyramid sale channel. Many of business operations are consistent with the socially beneficial from MLM model and inconsistent with the socially harmful pyramid scheme model. Applying on economic test that requires member performance payment incentives to be primarily funded out of retail based product sales to be classified as a legitimate MLM, based on prior test, at least 62% of total life or eating product purchases would need to be retail based online sale channel. However, multi level marketing is a mulit million dollar global industry. There exists differentiating a valid mulit level marketing scheme and pyramid money circulation scheme. Multi level or network marketing is a form of business that uses independent representatives to sell products or services to family or friends etc. It is a business strategy, which involves participants at various levels, the level above getting returns at the levels below it. Basically, it works on the principle of duplication to increase retail or sale activity. The survival of the system, depends on the chain of earns commissions from retail sales who makes, and also from retail sales made by other people who recruit.

Direct selling organizations can be of various types, multi level format, network hierarchal structure or the organization can be flat. Multi level marketing activity is a method of distributing products or services in which is from distributrs. MLM has these characteristics: the presence of sponsorship lines that create financial rewards between distributors. Suppose x recruits y, x becomes y's sponsor and distributors. Suppose x immediate upline y recruits z, z who as personal recuits of y, and x are y's frontline people (z, t and u) recruited by same sponsor y and on same level and members of the same generation (z, t and u) sponsorship lines seem like family trees. In fact, these sponsors are often called genealogies. Suppose persons s and y are both recruited/sponsored by x. However, y has been more aggressive, heavily recruiting than s. y will become more financially successful than s, even through they are on the same level and had entered the business together. The higher the sales a group generates, the higher would be the amount of commission received by x. There are numerous recognition levels, for example, Amway has various levels of recognition, each with its own unique title and perks. One begins as a basic distributor, works whose way up through the ranks from silver producer to gold distributor to platinum direct distributor to Ruby direct distributors climbing up the ladder to crown direct distributor to crown ambassador direct distributor. But none of the levels and title is authoritative. In MLM schemes, the uplines are paid commissions and bonus on the sales made by their respective downline members. The company using multi level marketing method is a MLM company. The MLM company can be a firm, an individual corporation or other business entity, e.g. Amway, Mark Kay, Modicare etc. MLM entities. It's features include word of mouth sales, means savings on marketing and advertising costs, company can change their similar products in stores, the technique develops loyal customers who enjoy buying from other people who know. It is such a pyramid scheme " which concentrates on the commissions, the participant could earn just for recruiting new distributors" and which generally ignore the marketing and selling of products and services. Pyramid scheme means any sales device or plan under which a person gives consideration to another person in exhange for compensation as the right to receive compensation which is derived primarily from the introduction of other persons into the sale device or plan rather than from the sale of products or services or other property. Pyramid means a multi layered network of subscribers to be a form by subscribers enrolling one or more subscribers in order to receive any money benefits directly or indirectly, as a result of enrollment. It is similar to a continuous chain of participants or investors is recuited, in which each pays a fee to participate and receives money by recruiting others into the system. So each participant can build multi layered network of individuals to have chance to earn more benefit, if who can distribute products to sell successful from whose downline recuriters network.

Finally, the main question is whether this MLM network sale method can assist any country economic growth. I shall analyze what the difference of social effects (influences) are from these kind of sale methods, such as direct personal sale and auto online sale and multi level (network) sale. A phenomenon appears that the distribution companies accept normal direct personal selling method to cause education expenditure to bring loss their bases of values all at once. It comes a lot of direct sellers are lost to any countries. Due to it raise the compensation to the choice of direct personal sale companies. For example, China government achieves laws and policies to stop direct personal sale scheme companies to enter to local market to sell their products. Because China decides to protect its local businesses benefits to let them have ability to sell their products, due to reducing the number of growing foreign direct personal sale scheme companies exist in China itself country. Although, China will reduce GDP income from foreign direct personal import sale. But it can protect its local businessmen benefits to reduce competition. Otherwise, Multi level (network) marketing is a marketing approach that can motivate its participants to promote a certain product among their friends. It can exist in one form before in the internet age began, such as pyramid scheme. Social networks are everywhere, our email and phone address books, our famil relatives etc. Social network has web-based form, as facebook, twitter, linkedin networks made them more tangible. Moreover, internet can be good sale channel for multi level market, it gives the potential to accumulate small rewards from each participant to a sizable sum, as internet channel can allow advertisers to attract early adopters to earn commissions when the advertisers can help any multi level market companies to sell products successfully from internet channel. So, online advertisers and participants or distributors who can earn profit from multi level marketing. It seems Multi level marketing can give chance to let any participants to buid many downline recruiters to assist the team leader to sell many products from internet channel. So, the team leaders and team members do not need capital to set up their businesses and who can do business with the MLM company together easily from internet channel.

MLM or network market is often compared such as direct sales e.g. insurance, franchises etc. In fact, it is in the nature of pyramid schemes for the money to go to the person at the top of a pyramid of participants, with the majority of participants found to be in a losing position at the bottom regardless of when it collapses or is terminated. So, the compensation plan can be considered product-based pyramid schemes or recruiting MLM's because their compensation plan rewards recruiting of distributors through commission from their purchases more than selling direct to consumers. Distributors must not need to purchase products from the MLM in order to participate in the business. These findings raise some important questions: what kind of business has no clients? Only MLM's pretending to be direct sellers. Who is buying the products that can earn income from different countries residents online sale channel. Only MLM's distributors and advertisers are their main customers. If there are no direct sales to speak of, then who is making profits of these supposed sales. Only MLM company founders and officers. Whether multi level marketing can be potential tool for socio-economic development. For example, insurance business is just one among them. Selling insurance policies can operate from internet channel conveniently, traditionally is considered as a job or business. With the competition raises in industry sector, companies are looking for innovative methods to spread the message and maximum business in shorter time. Many local MLM companies have quite large spread in the market, as joining with leading insurance brands to promise life product policy protection to reduce clients' risk loss from internet MLM sale method. So, insurance sector makes online MLM route provides employment opportunities of people and enhances their social status. This multiple role of MLM companies can be looked at as a social contribution and which can develop oriented social movement.

In conclusion, MLM can raise employment generation, mobilizing long term funds and improving quality of life of people. In traditional, successful personal selling based on referrals is the key to ensure regular expansion of client base and building long term client relation. A country like India offers well run MLM online marketing networks to promote consumer products. Conveniently online MLM marketing may become slow or stagnated over a period of time. Online, Multi level marketing may be the tool in such situation, India has many people, so the online multi level businesses can be built to attempt to operate in this country. Concept selling mostly used personal selling as a tool where the sales people depend on referrals. In MLM technically, e.g. online sale, the promotion expenditures on advertisments channel margins etc. is distributed among the participants as individual product distributors or product advertisers , as who can do online business from commission incentives to build businesses from internet.

Hence, internet technology can raise MLM to have competitive advantage. For example, it is common knowledge that MLM works on the concept of time leverage. A work to be done by you 100 days can be completed in one day if you have 100 people under you in a chain doing one days work. You can earn a % of incentive for the work done by each of those 100 people under your team downline. Through it is given various names like network marketing, freelance network chain marketing. To conclude, MLM can assist any countries economic growth to compare other kind of sale methods easily in the short time in possible.

CHAPTER FOUR

Organizational Behavior

Q1 How facility management influences airport and logistic organizational employee performance ?

● Facility management assists employees reduce
maintenance service expenditure

Facility management provides a variety of non core operations and maintenance services to support any organizations' operation. For logistic organization example, it is possible to provide effective maintenance service to warehouse in order to reduce warehouse facilities to be damaged to bring to spend to buy any new equipment facilities expenditure. So, when the logistic company's warehouse facilities can be maintenance to be the best quality. Then, they can be used these warehouses' machines facilities again. Their performance can assist workers to manufacture any products to keep the most efficiently an raising the best production performance in whole manufacturing process. Then, this logistic company's facility management department can bring to avoid purchase any new machine facilities expenditure spending. One to these warehouses' production machine facilities are kept in the best production performance environment even in long term production need.

I shall indicates airport and warehouse facilities how to influence employees performances as below:

(1) How can comfortable warehouse facilities influence workers' efficiencies in logistic industry ?

The logistic industry's facility management department can create cost savings and efficiency of the warehouse's workplaces. It's machines facilities (production machines) are dealt with the maintenance management of the physical assets maintenance service. FM (facilities management) has been being applied to industrial facilities in logistic and warehouse industry long term as well as maintenance plays a significant role to ensure the full service and the warehousing system, including both building components and equipment in warehouse.

Maintenance service is needed to bring a certain level of availability and reliability of a warehouse facilities system and its components and its ability perform to a standard level of quality. So , it seems that logistic industry's warehouse asset cost reducing. It depends on whether it has one facility management department to provide maintenance service to itself warehouse workplace's production machine facilities and warehouse building itself in order to let workers t feel the manufacturing machines can bring good manufacturing performance to assist them to produce any products in one safe warehouse workplace environment. Hence, the performance measurement of warehouse maintenance issue will be valued to be consider to every warehouse manager and facility manager in logistic industry.

In logistic industry, (FM) works at two level on the one hand, it provides a safe and efficient working environment, which is essential to influence warehouse workers whether how they perform to do their manufacturing tasks or logistic goods delivery tasks in warehouse. When they feel the warehouse is safe environment to work. They will not need to consider anywhere has risk to cause they die by accident in warehouse. Hence, they can concentrate on doing their every tasks . On the other hand, it can involve strategic issues, such as property (warehouse workplace and management, strategy property decision and warehouse facility, e.g. manufacturing machine, facility maintenance and checking planning and maintenance planning development.

However, reducing the operating expense issue will be the main aim when the logistic company feels that it has need to set up one in-house facility management department to carry on any maintenance service for its warehouses' any workplace property and manufacturing machines facilities. So, when the logistic company decides to implement one facility management department, it needs to ensure its facility management department can bring the minimum level of keeping manufacturing performance and efficiency to its warehouses' any manufacturing machines and warehouses' property to avoid to be damaged in short term, such as loss of business due to failure in service, provision of project to customer satisfaction, provision of safe environment, effective utilisation of workplace space, e.g. warehouse effectiveness and communication between the workers and the logistic managers in the warehouse workplace , due to the warehouse's space is not enough maintenance service reliability to the logistic company's warehouse, responsiveness of the warehouse's worker individual negative emotion problem, due to he/she often feels need to work in one unsafe warehouse working environment. Hence, it seems that poor or unsafe warehouse working environment can influence workers feel negative emotion to work to bring low efficiency (inefficiency) or under productive performance in warehouse. It has relationship to influence they to bring psychological negative emotion feeling to work when the organization lacks one effective warehouse management repairing service to be provided to the warehouse's facilities and properties' maintenance needs in order to avoid ineffective measurement and misleading of performance.

Hence, the logistic company's facilities management department often needs to be reviewed whether its maintenance service level is passed to achieve the lowest repair (maintenance) service standard to its warehouse itself property and manufacturing machine or warehouse delivery tool facilities or warehouse lamps' light whether is enough to let workers to see anything clearly to avoid accident occurrence or see anything to work clearly or the warehouse space areas are enough to let they can have enough space to walk or communicate to their team supervisors or deliver any goods more easily in the short distance between the worker's sending goods location and the delivering goods destination in order to avoid because the lacking enough space to cause the accident occurrence , due to the space is not enough to let they deliver their goods to any locations in warehouse.

Hence, it seems logistic company's (FM) department can contribute to the organization's mission, such as avoiding warehouse accident occurrence, inefficiency, not enough and unavailability of the facility for future needs when the warehouse lacks enough space areas to bring poor performance of facility and dangerous warehouse itself property in warehouse, e.g. safe and reliable operations of material handling equipment and maintenance of warehouse facilities, grounds, security system, utilities, plumbing, heating , enough lighting system, air conditioning, warming heater, fire protection, security system alarm etc. facilities in warehouse.

Hence, it seems that if the logistic company expected to reduce to spend lot of excessive manufacturing machine purchase expenditure, lose of workers' life or bring workplace accidents , due to poor warehouse workplace environment, even bringing lawsuit compensation claim loss , due to the worker individual accident or death is caused from the poor warehouse facilities, or bring negative emotion to let the workers feel they are working in unsafe warehouse workplace environment. Then, it ought choose to set up on facility management department in order to provide enough maintenance service to its warehouse to avoid these non essential expenditure causing , due to these poor warehouse facilities factors.

Hence any logistic company ought choose to set up one itself in -house facility management department, it be better than outsourcing its all facilities service to one facility management (maintenance service provider) to help it to deal any kinds of maintenance service in warehouse. Because it is long term maintenance need to its warehouse's any machines and warehouse itself properties. If it chose to find one outsourcing facilitiy management maintenance service provider to replace its in-house facility management department to deal all related facilities maintenance tasks in warehouse. Then, it is possible that it needs to pay long time facilities maintenance service fee to its outsourcing facility management maintenance service provider more than itself facility management maintenance service provision department.

(2) Can facility management influence tourism industry's human resource management influence to improve productivity in airline, travel agent, hotel tourism sectors?

In tourism industry, measuring productivity froma HRM prespective is extremely difficult and has proven to be a limitation within the tourism sector. Due to the customers are not tangible. For example, how can the travel agent measure its travel consultant individual service performance to evaluate whether the travelling customer feels or does not feel satisfactory loyalty from his/her service? How can the airline measure its pilot , airline front-line travelling passenger service attendant indiviual service performance to evaluate whether his/her travelling passenger feels or does not feel satisfactory to whose service performance? Whether airport facility management can influence airline counter service staffs performance ?

However, the complaint number whether it is more or less to the airline or travel agent's service behavior , it does not represent whose service attitude or behavior or performance is poor absolutely because there are many travelling consumers whose complaints are unreasonable , although they feel satisfactory to the airline attendent or airline front -line service staffs individual service performance, but if they feel unhappy to be caused by the airline or travel agent service staff. They will still compain their performance. For this suitation example , it is possible that the travelling passenger is delayed to catch the airplance to fly, due to the country's sudden worse weather influnce, he/

she will complain the airline fron-line counter travelling customer service staffs, it concerns when the air plane will arrive the airport, if the airline counter service staff's feedback is that the airplane needs long time arrival. Then, the travelling passengers will complain to the airline counter service staffs in angry. But in fact, the air plane delays to arrive the airport, the airline counter service staffs ought not need responsibilitie to explain the reason why they can not assist the delayed air plane to arrive the country in easier. Furthermore, thy will be complained unreasonably. Hence, it is difficult to measure tourism sector's service staffs ' performance, also the complaint exact number is not one judgement factor to measure their service performance absolutely.

I assume any tourism industry's front -line service airline staffs, they must attempt to serve their travelling passenger in positive service attitude and behavior. So, any tourism industy, how to improve their front -line service staff performance in order to let they to know how to deal unreasonable complaints in sudden unpredictive suitation. Their training materials or contents my include: Teaching them how to provide positive feedback to treat any travelling passenger individual difficult problems or unreasonable complaints in order to reduce their psychological pressure to unknown how to treat these passenger individual related problems when they are facing in airports or travelling agent workplaces. The travelling agent or airline travelling service organizations can attempt to collect measures of employee performance from customers , for example, comment cards in hotel rooms, airplane, travel agent's workplace, mystery shoppers etc. more focus shouls be pleased on this form of evaluation. In order to evaluate the actually place value on the customer ratings to every employee. The all every day, the form of evaluation concerning the actually value on the customer ratings , will be gathered to strategic , it has how many customers feel good or bad ratings to every employee individual performance when every one's tasks are finishing. Due to one month, it can make statistic report to calculate how much performance marks to give to every employee in order to evaluate whether every one's performance is satisfactory to be accempted to the lowest level. If the employee's marks rating is low, his/her department manager can arrange a time and day to meet him/her to discuss whether which aspects of problems who feels in order to give recommendation how to improve his/her service attitude to let customer to give higher marks rating to him/her next time.

Hence tourism industry's service sector organizations need to have one training department to arrange courses how to improve employee service performance in order to let customer to give higher marks rating to very one as well as finding methods how to excite every front line service employee individual loyalty , they can increase their confidence to know how to deal sudden unreasonable complaints in effective and efficient positive attitude.

In conclusion, how to improve employee service performance issue will be any tourism service organization's HRM concerning problem. Airports need to arrange how to implement efficient and comfortable and available convenient airport facilities to let any airline service counter staffs feel enjoyable to serve their passengers. They need to know how to find the most effective methods to solve how improvement of front line employee individual performance problem in order to raise the airline or travel agent's quality of service to let itself further customers to feel its service performance is better than others. So, facility management has indirect relationship to influence airport airline service staffs performances.

In conclusion, to decide whether the company ought need or not need facilities maintenance service or either set up in-house facility management department or outsource one facility management maintenance service provider. It depends on whether its organization has how many facilities are used in its workplace, how many staffs are working the workplace, how much size of its workplace, its workplace is office or warehouse or factory, how long time of its facilities' useful time etc. factors , then it can decide whether it needs or does not need one facility maintenance service department or outsourcing facility maintenance service provider to help it to deal any facilities management problem in its organization.

● Facility management role in organization

When one company feels that it has need facility management service. It can choose to set up either in-house facility management department or seek one outsourcing facility management service provider to help it to arrange any facility management service need. However, this facility management role is only one for the organization. It concerns this question: What facility management maintenance function can bring the benefits to the organization? It can define that all services required for the management of building and real estate to maintain and increase their value, the means of providing maintenance support, project management and user management during the building life cycle, the integration of multi-disciplinary activities within the built environment and the management of their impact upon people and the workplace. In traditional, (FM) services may include building fabric maintenance, decoration and refurbishment, plant, plumbing and drainage maintenance, air conditioning maintenance, lift and escalator maintenance , fire safety alarm and fire fighting system maintenance, minor project management. All these are hard services. Otherwise, cleaning , security, handyman services, waste disposal, recycling, pes control, grounds maintenance, internal plants. All these are soft services. Additional services, might also include: pace planning, things moving management, business risk assessment, business continuity planning, benchmarking, space management, facilities contract outsourcing service arrangement, information systems, telephony, travel booking facility utility management, meeting room arrangement services, catering services, vehicle fleet management, printing service, postal services, archiving , concierge services, reception services, health and safety advice, environmental management.

All of these services will be every organization's in-house facility soft or hard services needs. So, it explains why some large organizations feel need one effective facility management department to help them to arrange how to implement facility services efficiently in order to achieve cost reducing, raising efficiency and performance improvement aims because one effective facility management control system can influence employee individual productive effort to be raised or reduced indirectly.

However, (FM) can be selected either setting up one in-house (FM) department or outsourcing its services to one facility management service provider to help the organization to solve any kinds of facilities maintain service problems. One on-house (FM) department is a team, it needs employees to deliver all (FM) services. Some specialist services are needed to be outsourced, when the service is on expertise in the company. The no expertise services will be outsourced to simple service contracts, e.g. lift and escalator (FM) department will have direct labour, but it can outsource some specialist to help it to do some complex facilities management service. So, the team leader can of can manage whose team staffs, such as maintenance technicians run low risk operations . Otherwise, the outsourcing facility management service provider needs to help it to operate high risk operations or maintenance vital plant facility management service. Anyway, it can set up in-house (FM) department to arrange specialist direct labour and outsourced (FM) services to more than one facility management service providers to do different kinds of (FM) services. One of these outsourcing (FM) service provider, who can arrange sub-contractors to assist it to finish any (FM) services of it's outsourcing (FM) services are more complex to compare the other sub-contractors (third parties).

● What is a facility manager's role to provide quality service to satisfy its user needs?

We need to know how quality can be defined in facility management and why it should be defined by the customer? How facility managers can find out customer (user) needs? What are the difficulties in finding out users' needs and in delivering quality services? Whether improving quality always means requiring higher cost?

In general, facility manager's major responsibilities may include these major functional areas: longer range and annual facility planning, facility financial forecasting, real estate acquisition and/or disposal, work specification, installation and space management, architectural and engineering planning and design, new construction and/or renovation, maintenance and operations management, maintenance and operation management, telecommunications integration, security and general administrative services. When the facility manager had implemented any one of these FM services for those user. How does he/she provide excellent (FM) service quality ot let whose users to feel satisfactory?

In fact, quality issues can not be considered without customer-oriented perspective service quality involves a comparison of expectation with performance. (FM) service quality is a measure of how well to service level delivered matches customer expectation. So, these issues are (FM) service user's general measurement level requirement. The (FM) manager needs to achieve these the minimum performance measurement level to satisfy whose (FM) user's needs.

However, (FM) service quality has three characteristics: Intangibility, heterogeneity, inseparability. But in fact, (FM) service delivered may be through tangible physical aspects, e.g. factory plant workplace building, machine equipment maintenance, intangible (FM) services, e.g. managing space moving in plant to let staffs to work, managing outsourcing cleaners to clean factory equipment. However, all (FM) service performance often varies, due to the behavior of service personnel. Hence, a well developed job specification and training can help to improve the consistence of services of (FM). Any (FM) production and consumption of many services may are inseparable and they are usually interactions between the (FM) client and the contact person from the service provider.

Hence, it seems that service quality is considered as hard to evaluate. In (FM) service quality, it includes physical quality and interactive non-physical service quality. Physical quality is tangibles: The appearance of the physical facilities, equipment, personnel and communication materials. Non-physical services quality means reliability: The ability to perform the promised service dependably and accurately; responsiveness means the willingness to help customers and provide promopt service to let user to feel; assurance mans the competence of the system in its credibility in providing a courteous and secure service and empathy means the approachability, ease of access and effort taken to understand customers' needs.

Hence, a good performance of (FM) manager , he/she ought satisfy the user's tangible and non-tangible both service quality needs. I recommend that he/she can attempt to predict what are the (FM) customer expects in each (FM) service needs. Then, it can make decision what aspect(s) will be the (FM) users major (FM) service need and what aspect(S) won't be the (FM) users major (FM) service need. Then, he/she can make more accurate decision to arrange time, human resource , cost spending amount arrangement whether when it ought concentrate on finishing the (FM) major service tasks as well as whether how he/she ought finish the major (FM) service tasks to be more easily, e.g. how to arrange staffs number to finish, how many the minimum staffs number is needed to be arrange the major (FM) service tasks, time arrangement is important factor, because it can influence whether he/she ought finish the major (FM) service tasks today or tomorrow or later in order to have enough time to finish other non-major (FM) service tasks. Instead of time management, staff number arrangement is also important factor , if he/she arranged the excessive staffs number to do the (FM) major services tasks, then it is possible that it will have shortage of staffs number to finish the non-major (FM) service tasks on the day. So, avoiding either major or non-major (FM) services can not finish on the day. The (FM) manager needs to predict when the major (FM) services and the non-major (FM) services which are necessary to be finished in order to have enough time and staffs to assist him/her to finish every day major and non-major (FM) service effectively. Then, the achievement of his/her (FM) major and non-major tangible and non-tangible services , it will have more chance to be performed efficiently by his/her managed staffs.

In conclusion, in any organizations , (FM) manager needs have good predictable effort to evaluate whether when his/her managed team need to finish the major and/or non-major (FM) tasks as well as whether how he/she ought arrange the accurate time and staff number to finish any major and/or non-major (FM) service tasks on the day. Then, his/her leading of (FM) service team can be managed to work more efficiently in order to satisfy her/his (FM) service user's needs.

Q2 How facility management influences public service transport service performance ?

- How (FM) space moving management brings employees efficiencies

There are interesting questions: How (FM) can bring value-add to avoid loss or earn more profit to the organization? Can it influence employees to raise performance and improve efficiency ? Some organizations' (FM) service need which is necessary in order to let employees can raise productivity.

It is based on these assumptions: I assume the organizations have completely either outsourced or in-house their (FM) facility management departments will gain more effect on added value than they have no (FM) function as well as organizations have a strong coordination with the (FM) department will gain more added value than organizations with a weak coordination. Organizations in the profit aim can gain more added value than organizations in the not for profit aim sectors.

In fact, any organization is difficult to confirm it has relationship between improving performance, raising efficiency and owning (FM) function in its organization. (FM) could have to do with the attraction of easy but incomplete indicators of efficiency rather than the necessarily and less direct measures if the effectiveness and the relevance of space moving useful management, e.g. whether building has the enough space to let employees to move to work easy in order to raise efficiency, whether the building has excessive furniture and equipment number and they are putted on wrong places to be caused employees move difficulty in the building in order to influence productive performance.

However, how to arrange space moving management to equipment, e.g. copying machines, faxes, productive machines, they are putted on the locations where have enough space to let employees to move to another locations. For example, the building floor has more than 50 employees, but its space is not enough to let these 50 employees to move to any locations to let them to feel easily often. Then, it is possible to cause they feel nervous pressure and they can feel difficult to work , when they are working in a small office space or factory space or warehouse space. Then, the consequence will be under-predictive efficiency or poor performance to any one of these 50 employees in this office or factory or warehouse.

" Facility management is responsible for coordinating all efforts related to planning, designing, and managing buildings and their systems, equipment, and furniture to enhance. The organizations abilty to compete successfully in a rapidly changing world." (F.Becker)

The author explains equipment, workplace internal space designing, furniture space putting location arrangement will have possible to influence employee individual productive performance or efficiency to be raised or reduced in the workplace. Hence, it seems that, in the value chain (FM) belongs to the activity part of the firm. To make the facilities cooperation with each office or factory or warehouse using space moving facility management. Facility space moving management must be linked strategically, tactically and operationally to other support activity to add value to the organization's office or factory or warehouse space moving management arrangement more effectively.

Thus, how to arrangement space moving management issue it will have possible to influence the organization's employee individual productive performance and efficiency in whose workplace. It seems that (FM) space moving management arrangement have indirect relationship to influence the organization's employee individual performance and efficiency , due to they need often to work in the workplace, if they feel moving difficulty , or excessive equipment , furniture number is putting into the small office, factory or warehouse locations, or they feel the office or factory or warehouse has excessive (a lot of) staffs number to work in the small space of office or factory or warehouse. Then, they can not concentrate nervous on finishing every tasks in possible. In long term, their efficiencies will be poor or inefficiencies or their performance won't be improved or causing poor performance in possible.

Instead of the not enough space moving and excessive staffs number factor, it will bring another question: Can enough information systems equipment cause a more efficient and improved performance to the organization staffs in the workplace?

I assume that the office has 100 employees and it has only ten copying machines. So it means that ten employees use one copying machine. Hence, it brings this question: Is it enough to provide only ten copying machines to average ten employees to use? It depends on other factors, e.g. whether any one of these 100 employees needs to print how many documents per day , whether the five copying machines' locations are far away to separate different locations or they are stored in one printing room in the office, whether the day has how many staffs are absent, whether the day has how many printing machine(s) is/ are broken to need to be repaired. Hence, these unpredictable external environment factors will influence whether the five copying machines number is enough to let these 100 employees to use in the office every day. Hence, facility manager ought need to spend to observe average their copying behaviors every day in order to make data record. Many employees need to use copy machines to print documents, average how many document's page number, they need to print, how much average time spending to print their documents, average how many staff absent number on the day. Even, if the all five copying machines are stored in the printing room, calculating the staffs number whether how many staffs need more than five minutes to walk to the printing room to print their documents many staffs need to spend five minute to walk to the printing room, and they have other urgent tasks to wait to finish. It is possible to influence their efficiency, due to they often need to spend more than five minutes to walk to the printing room to print documents. If there are many staffs need to often to print documents, but their printing task will have many time, e.g. 20 separate printing tasks. Then, they need to spend at least (20x5) 100 minutes to spend time to walk to the printing room to print their documents. It must influence that they should not finish the other urgent tasks on the day. If there are many staffs to spend much time to walk to the printing room in the least 20 separate printing time or more on that day. All the facility manager needs to evaluate whether all the five copy machines are stored in the printing room whether it is the best location decision or they ought need be separated to put on different office locations in their workplaces, even he/she ought need to evaluate whether it is enough copying machines number, when the office has only 5 copying machines. He/ she ought need to buy more copying machines number to satisfy any one of these 100 employee individual copying task need.

In conclusion, effective office or factory or warehouse space moving facility management will be one part task of (FM) function. If the office or factory or warehouse can have accurate equipment, machine , furniture number to avoid excessive or shortage number problem to cause employees often feel moving difficult problem in their workplace when they need to move to another location to work in office or warehouse or factory as well as whether the staff needs often spend time to wait the another employee to use the copying machine to print whose document or fax machine to deliver whose document. Then, it is not that fax or printing machines number is not enough to provide the employees to use in the office or warehouse or factory workplace.

Hence, (FM) includes space moving facility management to equipment , machines, furniture number as well as choosing anywhere is(are) the suitable location (s) arrangement to putting or storing these facilities in workplace as well as decision of the staff number and the workplace area size whether it has excessive staffs number to cause these staffs need to work in the small area size of office or warehouse or factory workplace. So, the organization ought need to decide whether it needs to reduce the office's staffs number to let them to work in another more suitable locations in another workplace. Hence, all these facilities space moving management and staffs and workplace size issues will be (FM) manager's consideration issues, because these external environment factors will influence employee individual efficiency and performance to be poor to cause low valued to its organization in long term in possible .

Q3 Can gather the choosing right data public transportation service station facilities asset and analytics, it can give recommendation to help any organization to boost service quality?

(FM) analytics data can be applied to public transportation service industry to be supported how and why the train, train, ferry , ship, air plane, underground train public transportation tools' time arrival and leaving information notice board and automated ticket paying machines facilities are putting on or stored any where locations in order to boost passengers to feel their facilities locations are convenient to let them to buy tickets and see the arrival and leaving time for the next public transportation tool from the information notice electronic board machine. So, it seems that these public transportation tools' station facilities locations can influence passengers to feel the public transportation service company how to consider to its passenger's buying ticket needs and next public transportation tool's arrival and leaving time information needs in order to boost its passengers use service quality and let them to feel better service reliable performance in any train, tram, ferry , ship, underground tram, airplane stations.

As these public transportation service organizations need to learn data analytics represent an opportunity for its ticket paying machine equipment facilities as well as the next transportation tool arrival and leaving time information notice board electronic equipment facilities anywhere the locations are the most suitable to put on or store these equipment to let passengers to walk to the ticket paying machines to buy the ticket to catch the train, tram, underground train, ferry, airplane, taxi, ship more easily. So, they do not need to spend more time to find these facilities locations and spend more time to queue to wait to buy ticket to catch the public transportation tool in stations conveniently. Instead of where is the seeking ticket paying machine location, where is the next public transportation tool arrival and leaving information notice time , these both issues will be any public transportation tool's passenger's main needs.

Hence, how to spend time to seek where the next public transportation tool's arrival and leaving time information electronic notice machine location and where the ticket paying machine location , these both factors will influence any passengers' positive or negative emotion causing. For example, if the passenger feels difficult to find the ticket paying machine in the large area size train station or /and he/she feels difficult to find the train time arrival and leaving information to let him/her to know when the next train will arrive the station. Due to he/she feels difficult to find the train ticket paying machine, he/she needs to spend much time to find any one ticket paying machine in the train station. Then, it will influence him/her to choose another public transportation tool to replace the train public transportation tool, e.g. he/she can choose to catch tram, underground train, taxi, bus, ferry, taxi, ship to replace train. So, it seems ticket paying machine and time arrival and leaving information notice electronic equipment 's location putting or stored choice will be one factor to influence the passenger to choose another kind of public transportation tool to replace train at the moment. When, he/she feels that he/she arrives the destination in the most short time. Then, the public transportation service organization (FM) manager has responsibility to evaluate whether there are enough ticket paying machines number to let passengers do not need to spend more time to queue to buy tickets to catch the public transportation tool in short time as well as there are enough time arrival and leaving for next transportation tool to let passengers to know. It will be their concerning issues when they arrive the public transportation service tool's station.

Hence, predictive passenger individual walking behavior can help the public transportation service organization to choose whether where are the most convenient and attractive locations to let the ticket paying machines and the arrival and leaving time information electronic board machines to be putted on or stored in the suitable station positions in order to let many passengers can find these essential facilities in stations very easily. So, gathering data concerns passenger walking behavior in the public transportation service any stations, which can help the facility manager to make more accurate evaluation to attempt to predict whether where the locations are common places to let passengers to choose to walk daily or where the locations are not common places to let passenger to choose not to walk daily in general. Then, he/she can apply these data of different locations in the stations to evaluate whether anywhere they will have many passengers to choose to walk or whether anywhere they won't have many passengers to choose to walk in order to make more accurate decision whether anywhere are the most suitable locations to let the ticket paying machines and the time arrival and leaving information electronic board equipment to be putter on or stored in order to let them to feel it is so easier to let them to find.

Anyway, calculating each station's passenger number per day issue is important to predict whether where , there are many passengers choose to walk or where, there are not many passengers choose to walk in these different public transportation service stations in order to evaluate whether where the stations' different ought put on paying ticket machines or time arrival and leaving information electronic boards in order to let they feel very easy to buy tickets and seeing the next arrival and leaving time information for the kind of public transportation service tool conveniently in the different stations. Moreover, if the station has no enough ticket paying machines number to be supplied to let passengers need to spend more than ten minute time to wait to buy ticket to catch the kind of public transportation service tool in every queue every day. Then it will cause them to choose another kind of public transportation tool to catch go to working place or entertainment place to replace it to on that day. Then, it will cause these passengers who often do not like to queue in the kind of public transportation service tool's any stations, who will not choose to go to anywhere of this kind of public transportation service tool's any stations again. Hence, in long term this kind of public transportation service tool will lose many passengers. Thus, calculating each station's busy time of passengers number , which can predict when it is the busy time and it can make more accurate decision whether the station has need to increase enough ticket paying machines number in order to bring enough supply number to satisfy passengers' ticket purchase need in the busy time.

In conclusion, gathering above all stations' public transportation service equipment facilities number, storing positions data and every station's passenger walking behavior data, they are necessary to any public transportation tool service industry, because these equipment number and storing locations will influence them to make decisions to choose another kind of public transportation tool to replace it's transportation service if they often feel difficult to find these facilities in its different stations. Thus, it is part of task to facility manager's responsibility if the public transportation service organization expects it won't lose many passengers , due to these external environment factor influence and it also implies cheap ticket price does not guarantee the passengers will choose to catch this kind of public transportation service tool to go to anywhere.

Q4 How Facility management influences employee Psychology to raise productive efficiency ?

● How to impact of workplace management on well-being and productivity

In facility management strategy, design can lead promotion, the value of offices that are enriched, particularly including warehouses, shopping centers to raise their market value. Moreover, effective organizations, such as raising powering workers when giving the effective design of office space. I assume that a good design of an interior office workspace environment seems a psychological department to influence staff individual emotion to bring positive power in order to raising productive efficient influence, such as in a commercial city office. So, it brings this question: How workspace management strategy can impact on staff's working behaviors in office.

In fact, office tasks general include various forms of productivity, e.g. information processing, information management and any clerical tasks by computerization. Hence, office productivity concerns how to influence each office white color worker applies computers to work in office. The office space can impact on white color workers' performances in these several aspects: feeling of psychological comfort, organizational physical comfort and job satisfaction and productivity, efficiency. So, it seems that office workspace design strategy can influence white color workers' working behavior and attitude and performance indirectly.

The office space management includes: how to removal from the workspace of everything except the materials required to do the job at hand, how tight managerial control of the workspace, and how to implement standardization of managerial practice and workspace design. So, these key ideas will influence how each white color worker's efficiency and productivity in office working environment.

For this office space design situation, a large unseparated small space size's space design can accommodate more people and so brings itself to economies of scale. As a result, space occupancy can be centrally managed with minimal disruptive interference from office workers. Indeed, many businesses now adopt a clean and fresh air office working policy because they have more employees than they have spaces at which they can work. This desks are either taken on a first -come first -served basis. (hot desking) or can be booked in advance. So , when a company has many employees need to work in a small space working environment. It must concern how to let staffs to feel more comfortable in order to reduce high psychological pressure to work in this uncomfortable working environment. Hence, it explains why workspace design can impact on office workers' performance in some offices. All these issues are assumed that empowering workers to manage and have input into the design of their own workspace, then the effective office or any working places space management will enhance wellbeing to bring workers' positive emotions and improving productivity. I also assume the space working environment design have relationship of these depend variable factors to influence office worker individual productive efficiency. The variable factors may include psychological comfort, organizational comfortable, job satisfaction, physical comfort and productivity.

However, office furniture , facilities will influence office white color workers‘ performance ,e.g. the room size whether is big or small for manage office worker, a high backed, comfortable leather chair is needed for office staffs to sit down to let more comfortable, the door and most of the walls need glass, the office room environment needs have sea-grass rug beneath the desk covering the immediate working area, the office also needs have plants and pictures, mail boxes, telephone and computer facility is needed. When one staff needs to send email or phone call or send letters or deliver documents conveniently. These office elements are essential in order to increase physical well-being and feeling of satisfaction to white-color workers. Hence, geren office and office working space design management is needed in order to influence white color workers' productive efficiency in long term.

- Effective workspace design can influence communication to raise productivity

Office white-color workers often need communication between their managers, supervisors, and themselves. Office communication extends from the way that a user experiences a service. An effective office communication can bring these benefits; Providing positive influence on decision making by presenting a strong point of view and developing mutual understanding, delivering efficient decisions and solutions by providing accurate , timely and relevant information, enabling mutually benefit solutions, building health relationships by encouraging trust and understanding between the high level, middle level and low level staffs.

Effective office communication needs to clearly communicate its nature and purpose. Good communication ensures that all service staffs are sending out the same messages. Communication is also important for ensuring the service understands what users requires and why he/she talks about understanding users‘ needs and communication receiver can have effective communication skill to understand what he/she needs the another to do and the another knows he/she ought how to work by his/her task demand. Then, it will shorten much time. If the office has 100 staffs need to often communicate. However, if the office has good space management arrangement to let every staff can communicate easily and walks to anywhere to find the right staff to communicate conveniently. Then, they can spend less time to waste on communication issue. Then, their productive efficiency will be also influence to raise.

- Health and safe work environment influences productivity

Is a health and safe work environment can raise employees' work productive efficiencies indirectly? How and why it can influence employees‘ productive performance? Some occupations' working environments are easier to occur occupational accidents and diseases risks when the workers are working in the high health and safe risk's working environment. Hence, health and safety issues at these high life risk workplaces can be considered as a key to influence employees‘ overall performance. The idea that health and safety management program have positive impacts on productivity.

When one worker needs to work in this high risk of health and safe workplace. He/she will consider whether how his/her work behavior will bring suffer serious injuries for shorter or longer time from work related causes in possible. So, he/she will work carefully in order to avoid injuries occurrence chance. It is possible to influence whose work performance, low productive efficiency in order to avoid any occupational accident occurrences in the dangerous workplace.

If the employee feels danger when he/she needs to stay in the warehouses stable location to work often. Then his/her absenteeism day number will have increase, due to he/she feels that workplace accidents and occupational illnesses and can lead to permanent occupational disability, when he/she needs to attend the stable dangerous workplace to work in the warehouse. Hence, he/she will choose to apply holiday often in order to avoid injuries chance increasing when he/she needs to stay in the stable workplace location in the warehouse. It explains why companies increase need qualified, motivated and efficient workers who are able willing to contribute activity to technical and organizational innovations. So, healthy workers working in healthy working conditions are thus an important precondition for organization to work smoothly and productively. Hence, a health and safety workplace environment can bring these benefits to organizations as below:

It can prevent among workers of learning work, due to health problems caused by their working conditions, the protection of workers in their employment from risks resulting from factors adverse to health. The placing and maintenance of the worker in an occupational, environment adapted to his/her physiological and psychological, capabilities, mental , physical and social conditions of workplace and adequacy of health and safety measures are needed to any employees in order to bring positive impact not only on safety and health performance, but also productivity. However, identifying and quantifying these effects will difficult to be measured as well as the quality of a working environment has a strong influence on productive efficiency.

For one aviation air plane manufacturing factory, where workplace can environment will have high risk to occur occupational related accidents to cause employees' injuries. Hence, employees will be consider themselves safety when they need to work in high accident occurrence workplace. The bad consequence will influence such as absenteeism day number increases, leaving this kind of aviation air plane job of employees number increases, low productive efficiencies, due to there are many proficient experienced employees who choose leave this kind of high accident risk occupation.

Consequently, any high accident occurrence risk workplace environment , employers need have good safe and health strategy to let their employees have confidence to work in this kind of high risk accident occurrence workplace if they expect low productive efficiencies effect is caused by high accident occurrence risk workplace factor.

Q5 Is empowerment one good method to raise employee himself/herself effort in order to improve productive efficiency in organizations ?

Empowerment often consists of support groups, e.g. management's effective leading or trainer's training, course educational opportunities. Employee self-management education may impact to improve himself/herself job performance, e.g. increased self-empowerment, self-management skills and job treatment satisfaction.

Only organization's empowerment strategy can lead every employee to through improvements in the employee individual decision making efficacy, improvement task performance behavior by reviewing whether what are the employee himself/herself errors when he/she encounters any job difficulties, after he/she reviewed his/her task error and his/her manager feels his/her performance can be improved. Then, it can enhance satisfaction with the employee and his/her manage relationship and better access and raising efficient performance in possible . Hence, empowerment can let every employee to discover whether what task related difficulties he/she faces or encounters every day. When his/her manager give ideas to let him/her to know how he/she ought review his/her task error in a supportive education working environment, it aims to let the low performance or low inefficient employees to increase confidence to continue work in the organization. So, the employee turnover number will decrease , if the inefficient employees can feel that they can attempt to solve their task-related difficulties successfully by themselves. So, empowerment can increase social support, leadership and advocacy development , it has resulted in greater employee individual performance psychological empowerment, autonomy and authority to let every employee to feel to achieve to improve themselves efficiencies more effectively in any organizations.

For hospital organizational efficiency measurement empowerment influence case, how empowerment can influence hospital's efficiency raising? Efficiency is one of the most important indicators of hospital performance evaluation. Why do some hospitals' efficiencies poor? It is possible that mis management of resources, lacking health plan packages, e.g. coverage of basic health insurance, poor quality of care service, more payment demand for out-of pocket payment , quality of primary healthcare , healthcare providers neglect to concern potentially about service efficiency issues.

In fact, low hospital efficiency is the major problem to influence patients number to choose the hospital's medical service, e.g. when the hospital often needs patients to queue to wait for doctor's care medical service. They need to wait on hour at least or more when the hospital has many patients are waiting for its medical service. Then, it will influence them to choose another hospital to replace it , if the hospital 's medical fee is cheaper and it does not need patients to spend long time to queue to wait its medical service. So, service efficiency is important to influence patients consumers' positive or negative feeling to choose the hospital's medical service. Even, the hospital's doctors are famous or they own many medical working experience, if patients often need long time to queue to wait its medical service . Then, it will cause its patients number to be reduced .

These are variable factors to influence the hospital's inefficiency. They may include old speed hospital information system and medical record documents based on inefficient input and output variables. Input variables may include the number of hospital admissions, the number of nurses and the number of available beds. The output variable may include average of length of stay and bed turnover interval inefficient paper document record in the patient record administrative department.

However, to evaluate the hospital efficiency indicators may include technical, scale and managerial efficiency the out-based data development analysis approach and the variable returns to scales assumption was used. Based on the out-input based approach (maximizing the factors of medical service production), to increase efficiency the organization

should be increased outputs.
Hence, when the hospital has good efficient evaluation method to measure every staff's performance , e.g. ward administrative clerk, patient registration clerk etc. Then, it can base on an put-put based approach and assuming a variable return to scale, there is capacity to improve technical efficiency and managerial efficiency in these any hospital different administrative units without an increase in costs and use of same amount of resources in relation to technical efficiency and managerial efficiency and scale efficiency of hospital's administrative labour individual task.
In conclusion, factors, such as modification of managerial practices, use of modern technologies tailored to the cultural, political and formulation of clinical guidelines to standardize the medical processes in order to reduce medical errors and increase the empowerment of health care buyers (insurance organizations), length of stay, management hospitals by specialist managers, administrative requirement, full time hospital physicians, limiting the authority of decision makers in relation to the recruitment of staff in accordance with the needs of the hospital and optimal allocation of beds, conducting economic evaluations and the type of hospitals ownership had an impact on the hospital efficiency significantly. By increasing the number of beds the hospitals efficiency decreases. Otherwise, optimizing the bed size can increase hospital efficiency.
However, the important factor to raise hospital overall staffs efficiencies empowerment is needed to let every hospital staff to review whether why and how himself/herself error is caused and he/she needs to review his/her errors to avoid to be caused from any negligence again in order to avoid patients' complaints again or reduce the patients' complaint number aims. So, empowerment of staff himself/herself error review factor is one major raising efficient good method.

Q6 Can organizational facility environment factor influences new and old employees long term performance ?

In psychological view ,in any organization's environments, they depend on the types of social and physical environment factors to influence employee personal behavior how to be caused. How and why does the employee select to do whose behavior? If the organization's physical and social environment is better, then it may influence its employees select to work hard. It is possible to bring productive efficient raising consequence.
In fact, when one new employee enters the new organization to work, he/she needs to learn how to adapt to cooperate with the organization's old employees to work together. So, it explains how and why organization's physical and social environment can influence the new employee individual motivation of behavior to work. In regarding new employee individual behavior by new employer's culture expectations as well as new employees need to adapt of actions that are likely to productive positive outcomes and generally discard those that bring unrewarding or puniishing outcomes by new employer's treatment.
However, anticipated material and organization environment co-operation outcomes between the new employee and the organization old employees' cooperation, which are not the only kind of incentives that influence the new

employee behavior of the new employee actions were performed only on behalf of anticipated external rewards and punishment from the new employer. In actuality, the new employee concerns considerable self-direction in the face of the new employer's organization's old employees competing influences. However, when the new employee has adopted an intension and an action plan. When, he/she works in the new organization for a period, he/she can't simply not back and visit for the appropriate performances to appear.

The new employee's new job goal will be motivated by enlisting self-evaluative engagement in activities rather than directly. By making self-evaluation conditional on matching personal new job standards, the new employee will give direction to his/her new job pursuits and create self-inventions to sustain his/her efforts for new job goal attainment. The new employee will select to do new task behavior to give him/her self-satisfaction and a sense of pride and self worth for the new job chance.

Efficacy beliefs also play a key role in shaping the new employees' behavior to do their tasks by influencing the types of new organization's activities and working environments, the new employees choose to set into any factor that influences the employee's choice behavior can affect the direction of employee personal career development in the new organization. This is because the organizational working environment influences operating in the employee how to select working environments continue to work. Thus, by choosing and shaping the new organization's working environments, new employee can have a hand in what they expect.

In conclusion , when a new employee chooses the new organization to work. He/she must need to adapt the organization's new working environment. If he/she feels difficult to adapt or accept to the organization's new working environment, then he/she will be influenced to work inefficient or poor productive performance , due to he/she feels unhappy to work the new organization's working environment and the new organization's manager will dissatisfy his/her performance and complain or give verbal warning to dismiss him/her. Then, it will bring the poor consequence to let the organization's inefficient productive performance effect. If many new employees feel difficult to adapt to work in the new organization. Then, inefficient productive performance will be influenced to keep a long term. So, it implies that the organization will need to change its organizational culture in order to let many new employees can adapt and accept this new organizational culture to work happily if the organization expects new employees work to raise productive efficiency successfully.

Q7 Can efficient and effective interview psychological methods improve organizational performance ?

In human resource department, interviewing and selecting the most right applicants to do different kinds of positions, it is one part of HRM function. If the interviewer need to spend more time to interview to decide whom is the most right applicant to do the position in one day, e.g. 50 at least , even more applicants number as well as he/she can also make the more accurate personal selection decision to choose the most right applicant to do the position after the interview day. Then, the interviewing process needs to be avoided to spend more time to choose the most suitable applicant to do the position within the day. It is difficult to judge whether whom ought be the most right applicant to do the position, if there are more than 50 applicants , they are needed to be interview in the day. The consequence will bring HR department can spend extra time to do the interview task, but it can have enough staffs and time and resource to do other urgent or important task at the interview day. It will bring this question: How to apply psychological method to raise interviewer's efficiency to shorten to spend extra time to do interviewing tasks ? I shall explain some psychological methods to attempt to let interviewers have more confidence to select the most right applicant in short time as below:

1. Behavioral interview skill

The interviewer can apply the actual behavioral interview method to let the interviewee to answer how he/she deals the matters, he/she feels that it is the best decision in order to judge and analyze whether whom applicant is the most suitable to be selected, e.g. describing the situation, he/she needs or the task that he/she needs to accomplish. The situation may be from a previous job, any relevant event, describing the action he/she took and be sure to keep the focus on him/her , e.g. discussing a group project or effort in the team; explaining what results he/she achieved, what happen? How did the event and what dis the applicant accomplishes? What did the applicant learn?

In the behavioral-based interview. the interviewer can need the applicant to attempt to explain examples clearly in order to judge whose analytical skill whether he/she is the suitable applicant to do the position. The interviewer may ask the applicant to identify some examples from whose post experience where he/she demonstrated top behaviors and skills that employers typically seek. To judge whether his/her examples should be totally positive, such as accomplishments or meeting goals, the other half should be situations that started at negatively , but either ended positively or he/she made the best of the outcome.

This behavioral interview test aims to review whether the applicant's every example answer, he/she can provide an appropriate description of how he/she demonstrated the desired behaviors. In the behavioral interview, the interviewer can attempt to judge whether the applicant has good imagine effort to mind any relatively small set of examples to respond to a number of different behavioral questions to satisfy the right example are applied to the right situations in the limited interview time. Hence, behavioral interview can let the interviewer to make more accurate analysis to judge whether whom applicant(s) has (have) good analytical effort to solve any work-related situational problems in the most reasonable way or attitude in order to select whom is the most right applicant to do the position.

2. E-mail interviewing in qualitative research

E-mail interviewing is another good interview method to select right applicant to do the managerial level position. E-mail interviewing can be in many cases a viable alternative to face-to-face telephone interviewing. Internet-based qualitative research methods may include online personal interview and virtual focus groups. However, it brings two questions: What opportunities and challenges does online in depth interviewing present for collectively qualitative data? How can in depth e-mail interviews be conducted effectively?

The applicant targets may be the top-level manager, advertising executive , sales manager. human resource manager etc. management position applicants. They need to answer any complex or difficult interviewing question by email in the limited time, e.g. how to solve one case study problem , how to give recommendation to solve the situation problem. The interview participants may be recruited by tool/method of psychological test questions, the interview questions may be interview guide in a single e-mail and follow yp, length of email data collection period may be up to 10 weeks, the number of e-mail or follow up exchanges may be several number. The electronic formal and require little editing or formation before the applicants are processed for analysis all e-mail interviewing questions. So, they need to answer any managerial case study problem in limited time.

It is one good managerial interview test method to evaluate whether whom applicant has the best analysis effort in order to the managerial position, because they need to find the best solutions to give recommendations to attempt to solve any situational problems in any un predictive case study problems. For example, when the applicant or a focus group of discussion applicants whom need to spend the maximum half hours to give recommendations to discuss to solve one complex or difficult case study problem either between the interviewer and the another interviewee applicant or between the group of five to ten interviewees (job applicants) themselves. Thus, after the interviewer sent the one case study question to let the applicants to know by every email channel. The interviewer needs to judger whether whom one applicant or one of the focus group applicants their recommendations are the most reasonable to solve the case study managerial situational problem within half hour to one hour. Then, the interviewer can make more accurate judgement to select whether whom has the best analytical effort to do the managerial position.

3. The effectiveness of motivational interviewing for young or older adult applicants selection process

How can apply case management skills to be effective to prepare any interview motivation? How to do the most effective and efficient to meet the objectives of the interview? Some interview techniques used may vary the based on the individuals involved in the interview. For an interview with the young age applicant more require a different approach than an interview with a senior adult applicant. The following are one pointers to assist with preparing for the interview as below:

Knowing the purpose of the interview and what needs to be accomplished . What is the expected outcome? Gathering all forms that need to be completed or signed having the interview and making list of questions that need to be asked, knowing the key facts and topics to be discussed, during the interview. Gathering factual information that may be helpful. Opening mind is needed in the whole interview process. Making an appointment for the interview and arranging sufficient time to set fully participate in the interview. Taking notes during the interview, let the participants know in general terms the reason notes are being made and how they will be used, opening ended questions invite the applicant to provide more information usually begin with other words who, what, where, how, asking one question at a time and keeping wording simple and specific, defining any terms that may be unfamiliar to the applicant , giving the interviewing participants in the interview an opportunity to ask their one questions or to clarify anything that was discussed, closing the interview with a review of the information discussed and facts gathered, reviewing any follow-up that is to be done by the case manager or others involved in the interview.

In an efficient and effective interview, the interviewer needs have good body and spoken word communication to the interviewee or the position applicant. Because a good communication can reduce waste time or avoid the extended longer interview time if the interviewer can make good communication to impact good message to let the applicant to understand what is the mean to his/her interview question. What he/she wants to know, the total impact of a message includes ,e.g. 7 % verbal (words), 38% vocal /volume, pitch, rhythm etc. and 55% body movements (mostly facial expression). The interviewer's body and verbal behavior can make more clear message to let the interviewee(job applicant) to understand what answers are he/she wants to know mostly. Hence, an efficient and effective interview can let the interviewer to control and manage the whole interview to evaluate whether whom the applicants' answers or feedbacks are more reasonable to be acceptable to be better to compare other applicants to apply the position more accurately.

Q8 What is organizational efficient raising actual mean?

I shall indicate construction industry case to explain technological factor is the major factor to assist construction organization to raise efficiency. For construction industry example, improved productivity could be attributed to advances in and increased usage of information technologies, increased competition, due to globalization and changes in workplace and organizational structures.

For construction efficiency, the construction process can reduce waste in coordinating labor and in managing, moving and installing materials, loss avoidance. It can achieve efficient aim. The construction productive efficient concept can be defined efficiency improvements as ways to cut waste and labor. So, one construction organizational efficient achievement means that it implemented through the capital facilities sector, these activities would significantly advance construction efficiency and improve the quality, timeliness, cost effectiveness of projects in construction processes.

On construction industry technological factor influence hand, it can influence that construction productivity how well, how quality, and at what cost buildings and infrastructure can be constructured, directly affects prices for homes and consumer products and the robustness of the national economy. Construction productivity will also affect the outcomes of national efforts to renew existing infrastructure systems; to build new infrastructure for power from renewable to renew existing infrastructure systems; to build new infrastructure for power from renewable resources to develop high-performance " green building" and to remain competitive in the global market. If the construction organization expected to achieve effficient aim. It ought consider how to change in building design, construction and renovation and in building materials and materials recycling, will be essential to the success of national efforts to minimize environmental impacts, reduce overall energy use, and reduce greenhouse gas emissions.

However, construction industry analysts differ on whether construction industry productivity is improved by efficiency outcome. They indicate construction efficiency needs to reduce 25-50 percent waste in coordinating labour and in managing, moving and installing materials. This is the most minimum standard efficient achievement level to any construction organizations.

What are the factors influence efficiency to any construction organizations? An efficient construction task process is made possible by a range of information technological tools and applications, including computer-aided design and drafting, three and four dimensional visualization and modeling programs, laser scanning, cost-estimating and scheduling tools and materials tracking. So, high technological tool will assist to raise efficient construction process to any construction organizations. It can help them to shorten time and avoid materials waste and control cost effective estimation for any construction projects.

Effective use of interoperate technologies requires effective team cooperative processes and effective planning up front and this it can help overcome obstacles to efficiency created by process fragmentation. Interoperable technologies can also help to improve the quality and speed of any construction project related decision making, integrate processes, managing supply chains, sequence work flows, improve data accuracy and reduce the time spent on data entry, reduce design and engineering conflicts and the subsequent need for rework, improve the life-cycle management of buildings and infrastructure.

All of these factors will influence whether the construction organization can implement efficiency in success. For example, interoperable techcholgies include legal issues, data-storage capacities and the need for " intelligent " search applications to sort quickly through thousands of data elements and make real-time information available for on-site decision making. How to improve job-site efficiency through more effective interfacing of people, processes, materials ,equipment, and information. The job site for a large construction project is a dynamic place, involving numerous contractors, subcontractors, trades people and labors, all of whom must require equipment, materials and supplies to complete their tasks. So, they need to know how to manage activities and demands to achieve the maximum efficiency from the limited available resources. Time, money, and resources will have possible to be wasted when projects are poorly managed, causing workers to have to wait around for tools and work crews are not on-site at appropriate time or when supplies and equipment are stored in complexity or difficulty, requiring that they can be moved multiple time (time waste).

How to improve job site safety and improve the quality of projects, significantly cut waste? The use of automated equipment, e.g. for excavation and earthmoving operations, pip installation, concrete placement, and information technologies, e.g. radio-frequency identification tags for tracking materials personal digital assistants for capturing field data. These high technological tool can help any construction projects to raise efficiency to process improvements and the provision for real -time information for improved management at the job site.

Moreover, on mannal research and development tools hand, instead of data technological tools hand, any construction organizations also need to consider how to take a variety of forms: How to test field on a job site? How to arrange lecture shows in efficient way, seminrs, training and conference, and scientific laboratories time, human resource available arrangement, spending expenditure budget to finish. Moreover, effective performance mearements are enablers of innovation and of corrective actions throughout a construction project's life cycle. They can help any construction companies or organizations understand how processes led to success or failure, improvements or inefficiencies and how to use that knowledge to improve construction products , processes and outcomes of active projects.

The nature of construction projects, the industry itself, any construction organizations ought consider the construction working environment how to influence construction workers' emotions. For example, when the construction site is high levels, of noise, dust and airborne particles, adverse weather conditions,and other factors that can cause injuries and thereby reduce efficiency and productivity. New types of equipment can make an active physically easier to perform, easier to control, move precise , and safer for construction workers. Similarly, changes in materials can reduce the weight of construction components, make them easier to handle, move and install. Manufacturing building components off-site providers need more control conditions and allow for improved quality and precision in the fabrication of the component, One study that examined the relationship between changes in material technology and construction productivity based on 100 construction a related tasks, the study found that labor productivity for the same activity increased by 30 % at least when higher materials were used and labour productivity also improved when construction activites were performed using materials that were easier to install or were pre-fabricated. So, it seems material heavy can influence construction worker individual productive efficiency in site, if the material is higher , then the construction worker's productivity will be influenced to improve (Goodrum et al. 2009).

Thus, the factors influence construction organization's efficiency. It focuses on whether the construction firm applies how advanced construction technologies to assist its construction workers to work as well as whether its construction environment can let workers to feel safe to avoid life danger or accident occurrence. When the workers do not worry about whose life safety as well as they can apply advanced construction technology to assist them to work. Then, their productive efficiencies ought need to be improved easily. Thus, facility management and advanced technology will be the main factor to raise construction workers' efficiencies.

Printed by Libri Plureos GmbH in Hamburg,
Germany

9 798886 298086